To Norman Leader   2000
   4407-37th Ave SW
   Seattle, WA 98126-2625

from. Mildred Dague
   168 23rd Ave
   Cumberland WI 54829

W9-BGG-432

HARDSCRABBLE

*Dean
Volevec*

Hardscrabble

Growing Up Poor in the Midwest

Dean Volenec

1998
Galde Press, Inc.
Lakeville, Minnesota, U.S.A.

First Edition
First Printing, 1998

Cover design by Christopher Wells

Library of Congress Cataloging-in-Publication Data
Volenec, Dean, 1926–
    Hardscrabble : growing up poor in the Midwest / Dean Volenec. —
1st ed.
    p. c.m.
    ISBN 1–880090–65–1 (trade paper)
    1. Volenec, Dean, 1926–   —Childhood and youth. 2. Farm life —
Wisconsin. 3. Wisconsin—Biography. I. Title.
CT275.V598A3 1998
977.5'042'092—dc21
  [B]   98–14063
                                      CIP

Galde Press, Inc.
PO Box 460
Lakeville, Minnesota 55044–0460

To my wife, Dorothy, for her encouragement
in completing this book.

CONTENTS

Acknowledgements

I wish to acknowledge those who made this books possible: My parents, Mom Hazel, Dad Paul; sisters Irene, Carol, Marion, and Shirley; my brother Merlin (Bud); our dog, Jimmy.

The author, January 27, 1927

Preface

Our 120-acre farm was centered in a community of conscientious, hard working people of Bohemian descent that had settled in near the small village of Montfort, Wisconsin.

Here, as children growing up in a setting nestled between the hills, surrounded by woods, and entwined by spring-fed streams, we enjoyed a tranquility of unrestricted freedom. Freedom to roam and choose any place and any time we so desired to stretch out on our backs and formulate exciting images from the slow-moving clouds overhead. Freedom to create our own entertainment. Entertainment that required we cultivate our imagination and build from this imagination, for we had no plumbing, electricity, radio, or television.

The few toys available were admired through the store window only. If Mom or Dad had to go into a store, where toys were sold, it was a thrill and privilege to be allowed to accompany them. There we could get close enough to the toys to see every detail and even smell the new, shiny paint that made them so attractive. The thought of touching a certain toy was a fantasy which became embedded and was relived for many days to follow.

Our family of Mom, Dad, four girls, and two boys did not at that time consider ourselves needy or in want, because many of our neighbors had less.

The beautiful, alluring hills and four seasons of climate changes provided an endless setting packed with interesting adventures that resulted in lasting experiences for this family.

My desire is that this book will take you back to this little community where you can spend some time sharing boyhood experiences with me.

A community of people hardly aware they were scarred by poverty and hardship to the extent that it became known as "hardscrabble."

FARMING

1

The author, sister Irene, and brother Bud

Our Home Site

Dad said, "Whoa!"

Jack and Ginny, the two faithful workhorses I was driving, came to a much wanted halt.

On this particular day Jack and Ginny were pulling our walking cultivator. I was about twelve years old and sat on an iron seat fastened on the tongue of the cultivator. It was my job to drive the horses and keep them from stepping on the small corn plants, while Dad walked behind and with two wooden handles, guided the shovels that did the cultivating.

I wondered why we stopped. Was it because one of the shovels had thrown some dirt and covered a corn plant?

If this happened, Dad would stop and uncover the corn. Maybe it was because we had covered a bird nest.

Ground-nesting birds would many times build their nest right close to a corn plant and before it could be avoided, dirt, thrown by one of the cultivator shovels, would cover the eggs. We would then stop and Dad would take out the dainty little eggs and clean out the nest and replace the eggs.

We were always told that if we touched a bird's egg it would not return to the nest, so it was always a challenge to note where this nest was located in the field. When we made our next trip on the adjoining row, I would watch to see if the bird was back on the nest. If I could find the spot, I could usually see the little brown bird concealing itself on the nest. After having this happen several times, I concluded that I had a secret all my own:

it didn't make any difference at all if you touched bird eggs in a nest; the bird returned to the nest anyway.

On this day Dad just walked back a few steps and picked up something. He rubbed it against his patched overall leg and handed it to me. It was a perfect Indian arrowhead made from white flint stone.

Dad said, "Git up," and we were moving again.

Driving horses on the cultivator was a boring job for a boy of twelve, so the finding of an Indian arrowhead was a welcome interruption in the dragging monotony.

As I fondled the arrowhead, many thoughts and questions crowded my head for answers. Had this arrow been used in a battle? Maybe it had once penetrated human flesh. Maybe it had taken a life. Maybe it had only been lost when shot at a bird or animal.

I could visualize Indians hunting all over the very land we were now cultivating. I became envious of the Indian. All the Indian men had to do was hunt and fish. Wouldn't that have been great to hunt and fish for a living? No more cultivating corn all day. No more milking cows every night and morning and getting switched in the head by their stinky old tails.

No more carrying wood and filling the wood box every night. Everyone said the Indian women took care of gathering the wood and water. That would be just great to have my sisters carry all the wood and water so I would be free to hunt and fish all day—every day.

Another look at the arrowhead made me wonder where the Indians lived in this area. They had to live somewhere close because Dad said that this entire field we were cultivating was once covered with trees and hazelnut brush. His dad had cleared it. This was not the first arrowhead Dad had found in this area, so the Indian hunting ground had to be right where we were working.

I concluded the Indians would have had to live near a spring. The only spring around was located right behind our big old two-story farm home. Our home was located on a small, flat plateau that butted up against a wooded area. It would have been a natural place for an Indian hunting camp.

In my mind it was now settled: where our home now sat was the site of an Indian encampment at one time.

This arrowhead find done wonders to help me pass the day as I fantasized an Indian life of hunting and fishing.

Neighborhood Talk

I f two farmers in our neighborhood were to meet around the Fourth of July, the conversation would open with, "Well, how's the haying coming?" From there on it would progress with the weather and other crops.

This conversation would usually extend into neighboring farms and an evaluation of them. A farmer's reputation was always under critical review and, but for a few exceptions, most of the farmers worked diligently to uphold this community reputation.

A good example was exemplified by a farmer's time of arrival at the local cheese factory. Each farmer hauled his milk to the factory himself. If the factory had fifteen patrons hauling to the factory, the first and last patrons to arrive with their milk soon became known around the neighborhood. The first would be spoken of admirably because, "He's up, got his chores done, and at the factory by six-thirty every morning."

The last to deliver his milk would be judged contrary because, "He's still in the barn milking when half the neighbors are already in the field working."

In reality, everyone was judged by how hard they worked. They were then neighborhood rated accordingly.

The farm wives were judged and rated also. If a wife was out in the fields working side by side with her husband, she was referred to as "a good, hard-working woman."

If a farm wife was never seen doing outside farm work she might never be directly referred to as being lazy, but you might hear remarks about her like, "It's no wonder he never gets out of the barn at night; I don't think she ever leaves the house to help him."

No favoritism or consideration was given to the farm wife in regard to the children she gave birth to and raised while still helping with the farm work. This, along with the meals, washing, sewing, housekeeping, tending fires and carrying water, was just something she was expected to do.

I can remember my mother helping with the haying and corn picking. When Dad would come in to unload, she would hurry to the house to fix the wood-stove fire and get something going for a meal. After the noon meal, Dad always rested for about half an hour. It was at this time Mom did the dishes and began getting something started for the evening meal. After the evening meal, she did dishes again and she never sat down unless she had some sewing on her lap.

She helped with all the outside farm work until my brother and me could take over some of her tasks. She still helped then, but not as much. I never knew her to ever miss a morning or evening milking unless she was down in bed. She did get some help with the household chores as my sisters grew up.

I am sure Mom was well known around the neighborhood as "a good, hard working woman."

A 250-acre farm was a large farm in our neighborhood. The roads all followed the high ridge, so whenever you went anywhere, it was real easy to see your neighbor's farm and crops.

Part of your reputable name in the neighborhood was based on how straight you planted your rows of corn. A statement like, "His corn was so straight you could shoot a twenty-two down a row and never touch a stalk," would be a complimentary statement any farmer would be proud to welcome.

It was just as reputable to keep that corn clean of weeds. This demanded continuous cultivation with the horse cultivator, and some farmers even had the families out hoeing and pulling the weeds. Thank goodness our dad did not demand that we hoe or pull weeds in the cornfield.

A farmer was also judged on how many weeds he had on his farm. This was mainly based on the patches of bull thistles. Dad always carried about an even battle with the weeds. When my brother and me were old enough to swing a hoe, we were given a dime a week to cut weeds. This seemed a never ending job, but a dime for spending in town on Saturday night was something we eagerly looked forward to each week.

When Dad found time, he would hook the team to the hay mower and cut weeds. The fields where the livestock pastured always looked so well groomed after all the straggle weeds were cut, but it was only temporary.

Farmers also judged each other on the looks of a hayfield after it was cut and cleaned of hay. It was degrading to have a hayfield dotted with uncut patches of hay when the field was cleared. This indicated carelessness in turning the corners and perhaps a dull mower blade.

All farmers raised some pigs in those days. It took planning and effort to have the sows all farrow about the same time. This was necessary for concerned farmers because the pigs would then all grow and mature evenly. A farmer was always proud to show his neighbor a pen of thirty or forty pigs that hardly varied a pound of weight apiece.

Stacking hay was done with diligence, for it would be a shame to have a stack settle in anything but a picturesque, balanced manner. This required some skill to pile the stack equal from all directions so that when it settled it would remain even.

A pile of manure in front of the barn door was another topic of conversation. It was well known around the neighborhood who hauled manure and spread it on the field every day and who just tossed it out the barn door on a pile.

Anyone who had a charge account or bought a piece of machinery on a time payment basis was also the talk of the neighborhood. In our entire neighborhood, there was only one person who was known to buy on the time payment plan. This was known because they did their shopping through the Spiegel company catalog. At that time, Montgomery Wards and Sears Roebuck & Company were the two big catalog sales companies, and everyone did their shopping from these mail order catalogs. When Spiegel came out, they were the only charge mail order catalog. Regardless of if the person had a charge account with them or not, the person probably acquired a reputation of charging goods just because they shopped through the Spiegel catalog.

Farming reputation was also influenced by the condition of a farmer's fences. If a farmer's livestock were continually getting out and into his neighbor's crops because of his neglect to keep his fences in good shape, that farmer would soon become the talk of the neighborhood. Typical party-line talk would go something like this, "Did you hear about Joe's cattle getting out the other day and eating up Ed's corn? Sounds like they were out most all day. They say Ed was really mad because he doesn't know if his corn will come back or not. Well, you know how Joe

Author sleeping with cats on cement platform in front of house

is about his fences. He just keeps patching and patching and the wire is all rusted out. 'Course you know his pasture is awfully short and I suppose the cattle are getting hungry."

Flies

One of the most annoying things on the farm years ago was the hordes of houseflies. They were everywhere and into everything. Their peak of pestering was in the early fall. They got so bad the cattle ran wild like they were stampeding. They put their tails in the air and bellowed in frustration as they tried to find shelter from the flies. They usually ended up in the barnyard, and if the barn door was open, they would go into the barn. They knew they could get relief in the barn because the first thing we did before milking was to spray the cows. Dad bought the fly-spray liquid in a five-gallon can and we would put it into a hand-pump spray. We then pump-sprayed each cow separately. The spray threw a fine mist and killed the flies almost instantly. The cows welcomed this relief.

This spray produced a bad odor in the barn that was present all during the milking time. The milking was done by hand and it was not unusual at all to have dying flies fall into the pail of milk while you were milking. They were strained out when you poured the milk into the milk can outside. When you were through milking, the strainer would be full of dead flies.

Mother carried on a continuous war with flies in our house. With six children around, it was a constant struggle to, "Shut that screen door tight behind you!"

Mother would buy fly ribbons and flypaper to fight a never-ending battle with these pests.

The fly ribbons were a rolled-up sticky-paper ribbon that you pulled out of a small container. As you pulled it out, it unwound into a curly ribbon about three feet long. It had a thumb tack in one end that you pressed into the ceiling. Hanging from the ceiling, it made a good place for flies to land. Once they landed on it, they stuck and could not get off. At the peak of the fly season, it would not take long for one of these ribbons to be coated black with flies.

The ceiling in our kitchen was real low and someone was always running into this fly sticker. It was always an unreal scene when one of the girls would get it tangled in her long hair.

The poison flypaper was purchased as small sheets of dry paper. You tore off a piece of this and put it on a flat plate or dish. You then poured water on it. There may have been something on this paper to attract the flies, because when they drank this liquid it killed them.

We were always warned to never touch this because it was so poisonous it would kill us immediately. I never heard of anyone dying from this, but perhaps no one drank any. It was marked with the scary skull and crossbones.

The problem with this flypaper was that the flies didn't always die on the spot. You might be eating your meal and one of these sick flies would finish his dying flight right into the middle of your plate of food. It was always stressed to us how poison this paper concoction was, so when one of these flies ended up in our plate, we were sure we would die if we picked it out and continued to eat the food. In most cases, what you had on your plate was what you got for the meal, so the area around the fly was discarded and you continued to eat what remained.

At night the flies would settle on the ceiling in the kitchen. Toward fall, and the peak of the fly season, that ceiling would be just black because the screen on the doors and windows was loose or had holes that allowed the flies to get in as soon as they felt a chill outside.

Mom would cover everything in the kitchen with papers and then she would spray them with the barn spray. In the morning, the floor would be covered with dead flies and I can remember her sweeping up a dustpan full of flies every morning.

It was not possible to stay in bed in the morning without being bothered by flies. When we were real small and didn't have to get up early, we would get under the covers to keep the flies from our faces.

I can remember trying to take a nap during the day. This only happened on a rainy day when you couldn't do anything else. I would cover my head and arms with newspapers, but it seemed the pesky things could always find a place to get under and start buzzing and crawling around on me just about the time I began drifting off to sleep.

Flies were especially plentiful in the area of the pig pens. Dad had a big wooden barrel where he mixed ground oats and water together to feed the pigs. This barrel would be just black with flies. We would take a light, flat board and swing it as hard as we could over the top of this barrel and listen to the flies rattle as we hit them.

Flies had an ideal environment with the presence of pig, cow, horse, and chicken manure present at all times and yes, they were even a nuisance in the old outside toilet that I am sure served as another ideal hatchery for them.

Sex Education

Whenever we asked where babies came from we were always told, "The stork brings them."

As children we accepted this, and the subject was not pursued any further. As we grew up on the farm, we were exposed almost daily to nature's sex education program. Birds and animals did not run and hide when they copulated. If the mood presented itself, they completed the act right there and then and they had no qualms about us watching. With chickens and birds, it was an everyday occurrence, so we never gave it a second look. Probably the first interest ever aroused in any animal reproduction was when Dad went to buy a bull or borrow a boar pig. We would then raise the issue of, "Why?"

When we were small, we were evidently given a brush-off answer but as we got older and our "why" became more persistent, we were told, "Well, if you don't have a bull your cows won't have any calves," or "if you don't have a boar pig your sows won't have any little pigs."

Again, the "why" would come up but the answer was always, "They just won't, that's why, now run along and play."

We grew up with observing the breeding of cows and pigs but again it was a common occurrence that we hardly gave a second look. I do remember that the most puzzling part of the entire act was wondering where the bull or the boar pig got the big long tentacle that he put into the cow or sow because it could not be seen when the animal was walking around. It just seemed to be too long and big to fit back into the animal's body and this really puzzled us.

We had one workhorse on our farm called "Darky." She was the favorite among us kids because we could do anything with her. She was not excitable and very affectionate. When Darky was not working in the field, we would curry her and feed her apples and sugar, and she looked forward to this preferred treatment.

One day we heard Dad talking about raising a colt from Darky. We didn't give any thought as to how this would be done, but we were excited about a new colt because this was a new animal we had never experienced on the farm.

Some time passed until one day our farm dog began barking his message of "Somebody is coming."

We ran out into the yard and there was a man walking down the dirt road toward our house leading a huge horse. We immediately started in with all the questions and were told it was the day we were to have Darky bred so she could have a colt.

My brother and me were just old enough to where we wanted to get into the middle of watching this entire new show. We were in the barnyard when the man and Dad came walking down with the stud horse. A pole fence surrounded the barnyard and Darky was on the opposite side of this pole fence. When the man walked into the barnyard with his stallion, Darky saw it and she began acting different than we had ever seen her act in her life. She jumped and snorted and whinnied; she pranced around with her tail in the air and she was wetting all over the place. We had never seen her so excited. About this same time, this huge large tentacle began emerging out of the belly of the stallion. We had seen enough bulls and pigs so we knew what had to happen next, but we had never seen two huge animals such as this and we did not want Darky hurt in any way.

About this time Dad said, "You boys better get out of here now before you get hurt."

We knew that we were not going to get close enough to get hurt, but one look at Dad was enough to tell us he meant, "Get!"

We ran up around the barn out of sight and stood there wondering how we could sneak a peek somewhere.

The upper part of the barn was empty and the board walls were full of cracks. We slipped up there and each found a nice wide crack to watch through.

They took the stallion up close to the fence and let the two horses get acquainted over the fence. The horses made noises we never knew they were capable of making. They tried to bite each other and carried on to such an extent that it was scary to two young boys. After a get-acquainted period, the two horses calmed down some and the men opened the gate and took the stallion into the pasture with Darky. The horses again became quite excited. Finally, Darky turned with her behind toward the stud and this huge big stud mounted her. The man managing the stud helped him guide the big flopping appendage into Darky.

They done this twice. Dad gave the man some money and he left.

We really didn't know the exact chemical process that followed to make a young grow in a female, but we did come to realize that this same act had to be performed between a male and a female to get a baby to grow in the female species.

We just normally grew up to know that humans were no different than animals and even though it seemed repulsive to us at that time, we realized humans had to perform the same type of act to reproduce.

This sex education by observation eventually quelled the stork story, along with Santa Claus and many of the other childhood fairy tales.

Day Off

A day off from work on the farm during the week was something you just didn't have. If you did, you tried to keep the neighbors from finding out about it because you knew they would talk about you if they were aware of it. Dad and my uncle loved to go fishing, but this was done openly only on Sunday.

Once or twice a summer, after an all-night rain that made field work impossible, Dad and his brother would get together on the telephone. They would talk Bohemian because the phone line had about a dozen parties on it and most of the women listeners did not understand Bohemian. They would discuss and make their plans for a day of fishing by talking Bohemian. Dad would then take the back road out of our farm so he would not have to drive past the neighbors and be seen. We were ordered not to tell anyone, and so they occasionally sneaked in a day of fishing during the week.

None of us kids were ever overly enthusiastic about eating the fish Dad brought home. In later years, I realized there may have been a good reason for our dislike of these fish.

The fishing trip to the Wisconsin River was a journey of about twenty-five miles. The road was crooked and slow. Most of the fish that were caught were carp and river suckers. When caught, they were strung on a line through the gills and hung back in the river. This always took place in the summer when the weather was hot. All of these fish died on the stringers. They were then usually put in a five-gallon pail full of river water for the trip home. Many times it was chore time when Dad got home, so the milking and other chores were done before the fish were cleaned. We had no refrigeration or ice, so I can well imagine many of those fish were becoming slightly decomposed before they ever made it to the frying pan.

Dad was very fond of fish, especially if they had a good fishy flavor. I can remember my mother always telling Dad to eat slow and be careful of the bones because he was always choking on bones while eating fish.

One time while eating fish, Dad began another of his choking, coughing sessions. This one became more severe than the others. He finally had to leave the table and run outside. When he came back in, he continued to have problems and advised us he had a bone caught in this throat. This happened to one or the other of us quite often, and Mother would make us eat a piece of dry bread, which would usually move the bone along. Dad tried this but it didn't dislodge the bone. He went on about his farm work but periodically this lodged bone would get into a position where it would irritate him in such a manner he would carry on with a coughing, choking session that would result in him throwing up his meal.

This went on for a couple of days without him being able to eat anything. Mother tried to get him to go to the doctor but he wouldn't do it. Finally she got so disgusted she made Dad go out in the bright sunlight and she looked into his throat. Far down near a tonsil she said she could see a small fine bone stuck. We did not have a tweezer of any kind around the house, so she tried every household utensil she could find, but they all ended making Dad choke and gag all the more. Finally she took a long, pointed pair of barber scissors. Fortunately, the scissor must have been dull on the end because instead of cutting the fine little bone, the scissor acted as a tweezer and clamped on the bone enough that Mom pulled it out.

After two days of unpleasant disruptions at every meal, it was a great relief to be able to eat in a normal manner again.

THE BIG SPRING[2]

Author rocking sister in front of farm house

Life's Spring Related Influences

We had no electricity on our farm so the spring played the part of our refrigerator. A large, steady stream of water rolled and bubbled out of a large crack in the limestone hillside. A small excavation had been dug adjacent to where this water came out of the hill and this was all covered with a small corrugated tin building. The building had a lopsided wooden door with a big wire hook worn shiny from continuous use. As you stepped inside the spring house, you had to be careful to step on a plank. This plank stretched from a crooked cement footing under the door to a large flat-rock area where the spring erupted out of the hill. By standing on the plank, you could easily dip a large pail of water from the excavated pool.

The flat rock next to where the water came out was used to keep perishable food cool. After each meal, it was the duty of one of us to take these perishables down to the spring house. Most of the time this consisted of milk and butter, and it would usually result in an argument among us six children as to whose turn it was to do the job.

I can remember Mother invariably saying, "Oh well, if you're going to argue over it, I will do it myself."

This usually resulted in one of us older kids feeling sorry for Mom and taking the leftovers back to the spring.

It was critical as to where things were placed in the spring house. The butter had to be placed just the right distance away from the cold opening where the water erupted. If it were too close and the butter became too hard, Dad would be unhappy through the entire meal.

On very special occasions, Mom would make a dish of jello. It was cold enough close to the outlet of the spring and on the rock to make the jello set up.

It was always the chore of one of us, not old enough to help with the hand milking, to be present at the beginning of the evening milking session to take fresh milk to be cooled in the spring. The milk from one healthy-looking cow was always selected. This was strained through a flour sack strainer and put into another of the useful little half-gallon Karo syrup pails. This was taken into the spring house and submerged as deep as possible in the spring water. When we were through milking and ready to eat supper, the milk was served icy cold and delicious. As the family grew, so did the size of the pail, but the reliable spring always done its job.

The drinking water in the house was contained in a white two-gallon enamel pail and matching long-handle dipper. There was an opening cut into a narrow cupboard just large enough to hold the pail. The dipper remained in the pail at all times and everyone, even company, used this same dipper. This dipper pail drinking method was another source of controversy between us kids. One was always telling on the other because, "he or she put her slobbers back in the drinking pail."

Interpreted, this meant the one drinking did not drink all the water they had dipped, and instead of dumping the remainder in the slop pail, (explained later), they had put it back in the drinking pail. In the complainant's mind, the entire pail of water was now contaminated.

We called this "running water" because it seemed that the pail was always empty and one of us was always running to the spring for more.

The spring was located about fifty yards from the house. You had to go out the back door of the house, then through the yard, then the yard gate, and down the curved path to the spring house.

I don't remember how old I was when I had to begin sharing in the task of carrying water. I do remember I was not old enough to lift a full pail out of the spring if I dipped it too deep. If I did get the pail over half full, I would then have to use both hands to try to carry it to the house, and this always resulted in me getting all wet. It also usually resulted in a spill on the kitchen floor as I tried to lift this up and into the slot in the cupboard. This was usually met with a "Why in the world did you fill the pail so full?"

You always had an answer, but from experience, you kept your answer of, "So I wouldn't have to be running back in another few minutes" to yourself.

The big hassle always erupted when the water pail was empty and it was, "Better get ready for bed, kids" time.

It was always a ritual to get a drink and pee before you went to bed. Maybe you weren't too thirsty, but when you went to the pail and it was empty, your thirst became increasingly miserable. You usually tried to stall around, but sooner or later one of your lovable sisters would be yelling, "Ma, there ain't any drinking water!"

This always increased your love toward them because you knew it would be you or your brother that would get the next call. We tried to keep a running account of whose turn it was to make that scary trip. The determination was usually simple because you kept a very good account of when you got the last pail like, "It ain't my turn; I got one just before supper."

We did not have the luxury of a flashlight and it was too much of a hassle to light a clumsy old kerosene lantern, so you went out into that dark, spooky, scary, old night by feel only. I don't know why, but nothing seemed to bother me on the way down to the spring. It was always on the way back. I always whistled on the way down hoping that would scare things away, but on the way back, with the heavy load, I needed all the breath I had to help me make it to the house as soon as possible.

The old wooden gate was located about halfway between the house and the spring. It hung quite lopsided and had a well-worn groove in the ground where it drug when you opened and closed it. It served the purpose of keeping the cattle out of the house yard. I always left it open on the way to the spring, but on the route back, I always jerked it shut and, as I made the final run between there and the house, I tensely listened for that gate to open and let through whatever was after me. It seemed I always breathlessly made it to the house just before the invisible monster got me.

Once in a great while, during the daytime, my brother and I would catch one of our sisters going into the spring house on an errand for Mother. The spring house was made entirely of corrugated tin. We would jerk out our ever-ready slingshots and on the count of "go," we would each let fly with a missile.

If you are inside a small tin building and it is hit a good rap with a fast flying stone, it can be quite a shock.

They usually came bounding out of that spring house like a rabbit out of a stomped-on brush pile, yelling for "Ma." We always made it a point to get out of sight into the woods and stay there until things cooled down.

The only time I really had any change of feeling toward the spring was when I was called in on a big-game reptile hunt. This would occur when one of my sisters made a trip to the spring house and upon opening the door, they would be met with a snake stretched out on the walking plank. This always erupted in a screaming display of emotion that even startled Jimmy from his cool dugout excavation under the lilac tree.

"I ain't going back there 'til that thing is out of there!" was the usual response.

I felt highly impressed to be called upon to rid the spring house of this snake. I imagined myself as a bold knight in armor being called out by the king and queen to rid the castle of a giant dragon.

I usually had to pick up the butter, pail, pan or whatever was thrown when the snake was seen, then make my stalk. Invariably, the snake was a tiny little garter snake seeking the cool comfort of the spring on a scorching hot day.

With the racket my sisters made, I knew the snake would use the nearest hiding place and that would be under the walking plank. With a rake or a hoe, I could usually hook them out and toss them outside. I didn't like to kill them, but always passed along the information as though I had.

Even though I always assured Mother the job was done, my sisters were not convinced and it would be quite a few days before they would go near the spring.

The spring had a two-inch pipe outlet. This ran full of water and the access flowed on the top of the ground. The pipe carried water about fifty feet down the hill to a stock tank. The stock tank was tilted slightly so when it was full, the access water overflowed on the ground. This overflow then joined the other from the spring, and the two continued on down the valley in the form of an entertaining little stream.

The stock tank was always full of cold, fresh water for the livestock. The continual flow of water never froze, and on below-zero mornings, the vapor and frozen formations from splashing water around the tank made a scene that only nature's own elements could create.

In the summer, when we were making hay and it was dreadfully hot, we would stop at the tank and submerge our arms clear to the shoulders in this cold water. We would have a contest to see who could hold their arms in the water the longest. Many times when you retracted your arms, they would be numb from the cold water.

Carrying Drinking Water for Dad

Our farm was many times referred to as, "the place with the big spring." I am sure this spring was a significant reason the big old two-story farm home was built into the hillside on this site.

As a youngster, it was difficult for me to understand why anyone would build so far away from a road or a town. In one direction, it was a half mile out a two-wheeled dirt track to the main road. This involved opening and closing two farm gates, driving through two hard-bottom streams, and winding up a hill through a thick woods.

The other outlet was three quarters of a mile out through the neighbors to reach the main road. Other lucky kids lived right along the main road where they could hear and see cars. They hardly ever got blocked in by snow.

This cold, clear spring water continuously gurgling out of a crack in the limestone played an important role in the farm operations; a role difficult for me, as I grew up, to understand. To me, the spring and everything related to it represented an interruption in the routine fun things.

I might have been deeply involved in guarding the mulberry tree when Mother would call, "It's three o'clock."

Sometimes I would not answer, hoping maybe my sisters would get stuck with my chore, but when the second call came, which was a little louder and with a noticeable amount of added authority, I would have to answer with, "Yeah, I'm coming."

This meant I had to leave the tree unguarded, go get the little tin half-gallon syrup pail, fill it with fresh, cold, spring water, and take it to Dad wherever he was working in the field.

Guarding the mulberry tree was important because when the berries ripened to a black color, all the birds swarmed in to feed. My brother and I equipped ourselves with slingshots, and using ammunition consisting of small, green crab apples from another tree, we carried on a continuous guard duty. This guard duty was carried out in a discriminating manner against certain species of birds. These birds were chosen through hours and hours of close observation by us because of their greediness. These target birds were blackbirds, blue jays, and redheaded woodpeckers. They were the birds we had observed as always trying to drive away the robins, orioles, waxwings, and other good birds, so they were our targets whenever they presented themselves.

It was seldom we ever hit one of these birds and if we did, the bird would just let out with a surprised squawk and take off in a little shakier than normal manner as it flew away. We were sure everything we hit flew away with a small crab apple embedded in its anatomy somewhere. Occasionally, we would hit one in the head. This would result in the bird going into a flip flopping, screaming exhibition of commotion. This usually sent all the other birds scurrying out of the tree while the injured bird, recovering before reaching the ground, would take off in a very erratic flight to go nurse a headache.

With the shiny little Karo syrup pail full of fresh cold water, Jimmy, our farm dog and my constant companion, and I would head for the farm field where Dad and my brother were working.

I could never understand why my dad could not take drinking water with him when he left for work in the field. All the neighbors would carry water with them when they left for field work.

It was a common practice when working in a field, if a neighbor was working across the fence in his field, each stopped his team of horses and sat down for a visit. These visits could last an hour or better and were always filled with laughter. On such occasions was when I would see the neighbor go over to a large fence post and there in the shade of the post would be his pail of drinking water. For added protection against the warmth of the air, the pail was usually covered with a few bunches of hand-pulled, long, green grass; but not Dad, he had to have his water fresh from the spring.

Once in a very great while, Jimmy and I would get side-tracked on our water delivery route. This might be because of a gopher (thirteen-lined ground squirrel) that Jimmy surprised and chased into a hole. We knew Dad carried on a constant war against gophers getting his newly planted corn, so we thought praise and glory were in line for every gopher we could eliminate.

One of Jimmy's greatest enthusiastic endeavors involved the digging of a gopher. Upon approaching the hole the gopher disappeared into, Jimmy would stick his nose into the hole as far as possible, then inhale great draughts of air from the hole. After several of these inhaling exhibitions, which assured him he could smell a gopher in the hole, Jimmy would begin digging. His front feet would go so fast they were only a blur as the dirt flew. When the going would get tough, Jimmy would bite out a chunk of sod or maybe he would have to bite, chew and pull a tough tree root that caused an obstruction in his very enthusiastic progress. Periodically he would stop and stick his head as far and as deep as possible into his excavation. By doing this he sealed the opening so when he inhaled deeply, he only drew the air from inside the hole and with it, the scent he was checking.

As each check brought him closer to the hot scent of the gopher, it also stimulated his efforts and progress. If a rock that he could not handle got in his way, he would back out of the hole and look up at me. With the help of my pocketknife or a sharp stick, I would loosen and remove the rock. Jimmy was alert to move back to his digging as soon as this was done.

Unless the gopher's den was impossible to dig, Jimmy usually ended the escapade by pulling the gopher out by its tail and with a couple of snaps and shakes, it was all over.

To a young boy on a big game hunt such as this, time was easily overlooked. The little tin pail of water, sitting off to the side in the sun, was all at once a shocking reminder of the original intent of this safari.

My dad was always very particular and critical about two things. One was the time and the other was his drinking water.

You could have set your watch with the time Dad started chores each day, and your watch would have hardly varied.

He was well in his eighties and many years off the farm when, on a hot day, I remember him sitting in his battered chair on the front porch of their home in town and saying, "I'd give anything for a cold drink of that spring water off the farm."

So it was that when Jimmy and I arrived late with his drink of water, we were greeted with a stern, "Where you been?"

Keeping my eyes on Jimmy and trying to divert some of my guilt by scratching my supporting friend's head, I sort of mumbled a weak, "I don't know." It seemed a futile answer. If I didn't know where I had been, just who *would* know?

Even though we had been successful in getting rid of a gopher, this would not have been a justified excuse for being late with his drink, so the gopher was better not mentioned.

As Dad took the pail, he remarked something about the water being warm. This was because he could see there was no condensation on the outside of the pail anymore. He always demanded that the water be dipped and delivered without any interruption en route. I was too small to realize it at the time, but the beads of condensation on the outside of the pail disclosed the amount of delivery time.

When we handed Dad the pail of drinking water, he would have to first spit out his worn chew of tobacco. He would then tip the pail up and take a large mouthful of water. This he would swish around in his mouth to rinse away any tobacco that might remain in his mouth. This stained mouthful of rinse water was then spit out on the ground.

Tipping the pail up again, he would take enormous gulps of water. As he did so, water would overflow the edges of the pail on either side of his mouth and run down on the ground or sometimes down the bib of his overall.

When he was through, he would then hand it to whoever was helping him in the field that day. We always had visions of the water stained with chewing tobacco and were careful not to drink out of the same side that Dad drank from for fear that side of the pail would be covered with chewing tobacco.

Regardless of how thirsty you might be, you never entertained the thought of drinking from the pail until Dad was satisfied. He was first.

Jimmy and I were always glad when the water was delivered because it meant we were free to do as we wished until chore time.

I suppose that is why I couldn't see the value of the spring because it seemed to always interfere with my boyhood fun things. I couldn't understand it when Dad would make a statement to someone like, "Yes, that spring is worth hundreds of dollars."

I used to think, "Heck, Jimmy and I know where there are two springs nobody uses down through the hollow. I wonder if they are worth anything?"

Jimmy and I kept these springs, as we did a few other things, as our own real secrets. We knew where there was a nest of bluebirds; a big, old, fat horny toad; a hidden cave; and a crack in the back of the old outdoor toilet where I could peep through when my giggly cousins from the cities were visiting.

I am sure the spring also had many undisclosed secrets. I am just as sure many of those secrets were related to the arrowhead Dad found in the field.

The Slop Pail

Every drop of water that was carried into the house had to also be carried out because we had no plumbing. A five-gallon pail sat beside the washstand in the kitchen. All the waste water was dumped into the five-gallon pail better known as "the slop pail." This slop pail, when full, was then carried down near the pig pen and emptied into a large wooden barrel called the "slop barrel." To prevent this barrel from freezing, it was kept in the barn during the cold winter months.

Ground oats were put in this big barrel and water added to make a sloppy feed for the pigs. This operation originated the term "slopping the pigs" which was used as a term to describe many undesirable tasks in those days.

The slop pail in the kitchen was a catch-all for waste of all kinds around the house.

Almost all the cooking waste went into the slop pail except the raw potato peelings. These were always kept separate and thrown out to the chickens. Chickens seemed to adore raw potato peelings and, having the freedom to run the barnyard, they would grab a potato peel and take off hoping to escape by themselves to eat it. Soon another would spot the one with the peel and a big race would take place. It was only a few minutes before the entire barnyard was alive with running chickens fighting over the potato peelings.

All other household debris went into the slop pail for pig feed.

During the bitter cold of winter, the pail sat beside the kitchen cook stove to keep it from freezing. Mother always had the kitchen stove warmed when it was time for us to get up and get dressed so we would grab our clothes and run downstairs and crowd up against the warmth of the stove. It was only a matter of minutes before this warmth demanded the urge to relieve our bladders from an all night build-up. This was also done into the slop pail. There were times when we were still half asleep and with the pressing urgency to go, we were not too careful with our aim. This resulted in a short squirt against the side of the hot stove before we got our aim corrected. The noise and odor would always stir up an uprising from our sisters, and it wasn't a very good way to start off Mom's day.

The slop pail was also used as a burp place when we had the stomach flu. If your stomach was upset and you felt like maybe you were going to throw up, all you had to do was bend over the slop pail and the smell and looks would soon get the job done.

A white porcelain pot was always available in the master bedroom but great discretion was supposed to accompany the use of this container. A path was always shoveled to the outdoor toilet and when you were old enough to run the path, that is where you had to go. The trips were short and fast during the cold winter months.

WINTER 3

Shut In

Winters were long and dreary on the farm. Many times we would become snowbound for weeks. The roads would become filled with snow and schools would be closed. We might not see any other person except our own family for weeks. When the snow was too deep to use the horses and bobsled, Dad would take a gunny sack (burlap sack) and walk the two and one half miles to town to get the few needed groceries.

We would sit by the window watching down the valley for his return. We knew the grocery store owner would have put in a bag of candy for us and although it wasn't chocolate covered peanuts or chocolate stars, we were delighted with the cheap, hard sugar candy.

It was always great to get as close as possible to Mom as she took the groceries from the bag because they always had that store smell we loved so well.

When the snow packed hard enough for the horses to walk on top of it without breaking through, Dad would then use the bobsled and bring more groceries.

There was very little need for many groceries. Mom required the necessities to bake bread, rolls, and cakes, but that was it. We butchered pigs in the fall and these were fried down in big crocks or smoked, so we had plenty of meat. When Dad sold the pigs in the fall, he bought ten fifty-pound bags of flour and two hundred-pound bags of sugar. This would last until the pigs were sold again the following year.

The flour and sugar were stored in an unused room in the upstairs of our home. This room had everything in it, including mice. The mice would chew holes in the flour sacks and get into the flour. They would get covered with flour and when they left the sack, the flour would fall off them on the floor so they had little white trails leading away from the flour bags in all directions. Mom had to sift all the flour she used for fear there might be mouse dirt in it.

When I became old enough, it was my job to trap these mice. Mom said she would give me a penny for each mouse I caught. There was no end to the supply, so I visualized prosperity.

I remember doing real well, but couldn't collect because Mom didn't have any money to pay me until she could get to town to sell her eggs. Dad would take the eggs when he drove the team, but that didn't help Mom and me because he kept any leftover change.

It was a good half mile to the nearest crushed rock road from our home. We had to travel on a two-track trail through the barnyard, the pasture, across two streams and through a woods. During the winter, Dad tried diligently to keep our farm road open out to the main roads. He would tie a walking plow to the side of the bobsled and by making the horses trot, he could throw the snow out quite well. This gave him two tracks to follow, and as long as he kept the car wheels in these two tracks, he got along okay. Invariably, the car would slip off the two tracks and into the hard-packed banks alongside. We would then all have to get out and help shovel and push until we got the car back into the tracks again. All of us had to also help shovel where the snow blew deep in the gates and low spots on the road. We always reached a point, sometime during the winter, when his plowed

Car of a friend visiting us on farm

out tracks would drift full of hard packed snow, and that ended the car transportation until spring breakup.

When the snow left, we had the mud to contend with for a lengthy period of time. The only way we could get the car to the main road then was to drive it there while the ground was frozen. This meant Dad would get up early some morning and drive the car over the rough frozen ground to the main road. The car would remain there until things dried up enough to drive it to the house. This might be well over a month or more.

When the car had to be left out by the main road, Dad would load the crates of eggs in a wagon filled with straw and we would all ride up to the car where everything was transferred. The horses were tied to a nearby tree and everyone was jubilantly on their way to town.

This might have been the first time Mom was away from home for a few months, and must have been a welcome occasion.

By now my total mouse catch had reached twenty-two and I could hardly wait for my pay. When Mom sold her eggs and did her shopping, she dug in her purse and gave me and my brother each a quarter.

Mom was not the type of person who could have given me that much money and not the same to my brother, so she said she had been giving him some extra chores to earn it. This made me feel good because now I didn't have to share with him. I would never have felt right having that much money without him having some also.

That was the most money we ever had and looked so large we didn't want to break it. We carried it around until it was almost time to go home, then we finally broke down in front of the case of chocolate-covered peanuts, caramels, and stars. We each bought a nickel bag of these mixed chocolates and took the remainder of our money home with us.

Indoors

Our old farmhouse, with no storm windows or insulation, was very vulnerable to the winter elements. The older children slept upstairs. The only heat up there was what moved up a very narrow stairway. Many nights Mother would heat up flatirons and wrap them in flannel pieces of blankets for us to put in the bottom of our beds. We would put our feet against these and they would help us stay tolerable until our bodies warmed the bedding enough to allow us to go to sleep.

These flatirons were what Mom used to press the few clothes that needed pressing. They were a solid piece of iron built in the shape of a rounded triangle. They were flat and smooth on the bottom and the top had an indentation where a separate wooden handle could be snapped on. The irons were placed on the top of the wood stove to heat. When you were ready to iron, you hooked the wooden handle in the iron and went to work. The temperature of the iron was always tested by wetting your finger in your mouth and quickly touching it to the bottom of the iron. Mom always had two or three on the wood stove when she was ironing and when one cooled down, she simply sat it on the stove, unhooked the handle, hooked it into another, and kept on working.

There were not enough feather beds for everyone to have one, so one winter Mom and Dad filled a large mattress cover with corn husks for my brother and me to sleep upon. This was fine, but they were noisy when we moved about and it took forever to get the darn things warmed up. By spring, they were shredded up into a very small amount of filling and this would never be in the spot you wished to sleep.

Many mornings when I awoke I remember seeing little drifts of snow on the window sill. It would depend on which way the wind was from as to how severe the drifts were or how much wind came in. It always seemed the east window would accumulate the largest drifts.

There was one advantage to not having storm windows, especially for my brother and me. Since we did not have indoor plumbing and the only toilet pot in the house was downstairs in Mom and Dad's bedroom, we would just raise the window and pee right outside. This worked fine in the winter. Dad did have screens for the windows for summer and when he put the screens on, we did not change our bedroom habits. We just went straight out through the screens. This was fine for a while, but it didn't take long before this began to rust a big, brown spot in the middle of the screen. It didn't take the folks long to figure out what was happening and that put an end to our indoor plumbing.

Many winter nighttime hours were spent playing on the windows in the kitchen. The kitchen wood stove kicked out a lot of heat and because there were no storm windows, the windows would freeze on the inside with a thick layer of frost. By holding a nail with a pliers, I would insert the nail into the coals of the wood fire through the draft holes of the stove. When the nail became hot I would quickly rush to the window and press the point of the nail into the deep frost on the window. As long as the nail remained hot, it would cut a fast path through the deep frost and I could draw designs that remained for some time. My sisters were repeatedly reporting me for playing in the fire, but the reprimands were of the kind you didn't have to take too seriously. I really think the folks were probably happy to have at least one of the kids quiet and entertained.

I would also break out a long straw off the broom. I would insert this through the same damper hole in the stove. As soon as it caught on fire, I would pull it out of the stove and the flame would go out, leaving a nice red coal on the end of the straw. I would use this coal to burn designs and holes in paper. It would take some time before this awful odor reached the other room where Mom and Dad were relaxing, but when it did, my paper burning art soon ended.

Winter Recreation

One thing about the farm, there seemed always to be just what you needed around to make whatever you might dream up for entertainment. Many times it was a task to get Dad to allow us to use what we wanted, but persistence usually paid off. Our recreational activities were always governed by the weather.

If conditions were right, we would get pieces of cardboard or tin to slide on. These would give us a more sensational ride on the hard crust of the snow because we would be spinning as we went down the hill.

Dad had taken some wooden staves out of a big wooden barrel. He nailed a strap across the top and rubbed the bottom of the staves smooth on the sidewalk. These were our skis.

We were gifted with hills right in our front yard, so we were always anxious for the first fresh snowfall. If it came deep and fluffy, we had to make a ski trail down the hill. Jimmy, our farm dog, was our constant companion. There were times though that Jimmy just didn't work into our plans and many times this was when we were building a ski trail. When we built a trail, we wanted it smooth and unblemished, but every time we went down the trail, Jimmy came joyfully bouncing along behind us, putting big, deep footprints in our ski trail. It was always a difficult time getting him to understand our wants and needs. He would eventually use the path we walked back up the hill on except when we fell down. I guess Jimmy felt, "If you can fall down and roll on the trail, I can come over and jump on you and lick your face or steal your cap and play tag with it."

As we traveled the trail, it became packed and fast. Each night that it froze it became harder and slicker and faster. We would play outside in the snow until the snow packed around the wrists of our sleeves and eventually made our hands so cold and numb that we could no longer pick up our skis and carry them up the hill. Many times we stayed out so long that the deciding factor to go into the house was having to go to the toilet. We could no longer do this outside because our hands had become so cold we could not unbutton our pants to do the job.

My nose continually dripped while I was outside and because the sleeve and mitten were a handy place to wipe, this area would eventually be frozen hard.

When we would give up and go into the house, our hands were so cold and stiff we could not unbuckle the old metal buckles on our four-buckle overshoes. Mom would have to help us, and many times we would have waited too long, and when the heat from the wood stove hit us, we might dribble the underwear wet a little before we were able to get the needed clothes off, making it possible to pee in the pot.

The wet clothes were replaced with nice, warm, dry ones, and then we huddled by the stove. Shortly our hands would begin to tingle and sting. Mom called these "chilblains." I am not sure there is such a word, but it was something used in those days to refer to this condition. It was very painful, depending on how cold your hands or feet had been.

Going to School

We walked a little over a mile to school most of the time, but when it got bitter cold and the roads were drifted full of snow, Dad would take us in the bobsled. This was a large box on sled runners that was pulled by the horses and used for everything in the winter. Dad would use it mostly to haul up wood and haul out the manure from the barn each day. When he took us to school, he would put in a lot of nice, clean straw to cover the frozen manure that always dirtied up the box. We were then covered with big blankets and by burrowing into the straw and covering up with the blankets, it was a cozy ride. All we heard was the crunch of the horses' hooves in the hard-packed snow and the jingle of the access chain of the tugs that were part of the harness used to hook the pulling parts of the horses' harness to the sleigh. Every once in a while someone would peep out and give us a report of how far we had gone. I guess it was a pleasant ride, but we always thought it would have been much better if school had been closed until the weather warmed.

The Telephone

The installation of the telephone helped to break up the monotony of the long winter and was one of the most exciting things that happened for some time.

The phones were large wooden boxes on the wall with a crank on the side of the box. These boxes were placed quite high on the wall and the receivers you listened into had a cord so you could sit down and listen to the conversation if you wished. To carry on a conversation, you had to speak into the horn-like projection on the front of the box. My mom was quite short, so Dad had to build her a box to stand on so she could talk into the horn. I am sure the phones were purposely placed up high so the children would not tamper with them.

There were probably a dozen or so parties in the neighborhood all on the same phone line. Each party had a different number of rings to indicate their call. Our ring was two shorts. This meant if someone wanted to talk to us, they gave the crank two short cranks. These two short rings were heard in the home of everyone on our line, and if they were interested, they could pick up their receiver and listen or join in the conversation. This was considered somewhat unethical and was called "rubbering," but was done regularly by certain parties.

Sometimes, when Mom and Dad were in the barn milking, and we were too small to help, we would pull a chair over by the phone and when it would ring, we would stand on the chair, lift off the receiver, and listen to the conversation.

The all-alert for a distress signal in the neighborhood was a series of short rings. When this was heard everyone on the line was to listen in and get the message from the central operator.

I can only remember this happening a few times. I can remember when it happened in the middle of the night and excitedly got everyone out of bed. Once it was my cousin having a chimney fire and all the neighbors rushed over to help. Fortunately, it was almost out without damage when everyone arrived.

The other time it was about twelve o'clock on a cold, below-zero night. The snow was so high that travel was by horse and sleigh only. The announcement was that one of the neighbors had gone to town in the afternoon and never returned home. The wife was concerned. A few phone calls were made and each neighbor was assigned an area to check out. I remember Mom helping Dad get dressed in the warmest clothing he could find. He then had to harness and hook up the team to the bobsled to check out his assigned area. It was toward morning when he returned with the news that the neighbor had been found and was okay.

It seemed this neighbor had a habit of going to town and on occasions he would get quite intoxicated. When he did this, he would drive his horses out of town and after heading them in the direction of his farm, he would lie down in the wagon or sled box and go to sleep. The horses knew the route home and would continue without any problem.

On this particular night, the roads were drifted shut and the horses, not being able to see familiar landmarks, got confused and off their regular route. They came up against a fence and there they stopped. Fortunately, the neighbor was covered good with blankets and, when found, was none the worse for wear. For some time thereafter, it was the talk of the neighborhood that if he had not been well filled with alcohol he would have frozen to death.

I am sure the installation of the telephone was one of the greatest presents Mom could have ever received. During the snow-locked winter months, Mom never left the farm. She was continuously busy with the cooking, sewing, and taking care of kids. She never got away to see or visit with anyone other than her family. We children did get to school when it was possible. Sometimes Dad did not get to town for two weeks, but Mother never got there at all, so I am sure the telephone was a welcome outlet for her.

I remember the folks talking about the over-use of the phone that was practiced by a couple of the neighboring women. When someone was talking on the line, no one else could use it. They had to wait until the other parties hung up. There were times you had to wait in line to get to use the phone.

I remember, on a couple of occasions, when Mom would break into the conversation and ask if she could use the line. This was not an uncommon practice and most people accepted it. You can be sure the other party listened to see what made the urgency of the break-in necessary.

The phone line was run on posts along the roadways, but many times it was fastened to trees into the farms' homes. This created many outages from falling limbs and trees swaying during high wind periods. Dad always took care of this part of the maintenance of the line himself.

The phone operated on two dry-cell batteries. Dad was always complaining to Mom about using the phone too much and wearing out the batteries, so she confined her talking to whenever Dad was outside.

When the batteries began to wear out, the person you were talking to would sound like they were many miles away. When the batteries lost all their power, you no longer could hear at all.

Whenever you wanted to call what they called "cross line" to a party not on your line, you had to call "Central." Central was a lady everyone in the neighborhood knew that took care of the switchboard. She would switch your call to the person on "cross line" that you wished to talk to.

Central was also the local information source. If something big happened in the neighborhood or if someone was real sick, you could always call Central and get all the details.

I can remember a party, not on our line, who had pneumonia. Every day someone on our line would call Central and get the latest condition of the sick person. They would then pass this along in the neighborhood.

Central was also the source of road and weather conditions for those who desired that information. This was necessary at that time since few people had radios as a source for information.

Even though the first telephones created a means of one neighbor knowing the other's business, it did establish an important bond of closeness among these rural people that progress eventually erased.

Dad Buys Some Fish

Dad was always very fond of eating fish and he wasn't too particular about what kind of fish. In fact, he preferred his fish to have a fishy flavor.

I guess that is why he took such interest in a fish market brochure we got through the mail one winter. He studied it carefully and found something in the brochure called "whiting" that seemed to fit his pocketbook the best. You could only order these fish by the box and only in the winter because they came by freight, fresh frozen. They were ordered out of Green Bay, Wisconsin, and it seemed a long time before the freight office called one day and told Dad his fish were in. I remember we were snowed in at the time so Dad had to take the team and bobsled the two and one-half miles to town to get his fish.

We were all quite excited about at last having some good fish to eat because all we ever had were the carp and suckers we caught in the local streams, and we kids hated them.

When he arrived home, he came in carrying this huge wooden box. He had to get the hammer and screwdriver to pry a few boards off the top. There were his fish, frozen solid in a block of ice.

The fish were frozen whole. They were all uniform in size, about sixteen inches long and, except for their mouth and head, they looked like the suckers we didn't like.

I remember Dad and Mom got into sort of a heated discussion about the disposition of these fish. There was no way they could thaw and eat all those fish, and there was no way they could chop out enough for a meal. Finally, Dad said he would take care of them.

He sat them out on our enclosed porch. This porch was unheated but faced south and when the sun hit in there, it warmed up enough to gradually loosen the fish. He pried loose a few off the top and took them inside and put them in water to thaw.

When Dad first opened the crate, we all commented on how fishy they smelled, but this was mild compared to how they smelled as they thawed out. This didn't bother Dad as he dressed them up for the frying pan.

Poor Mom was pregnant at the time, and she was having a terrible time coping with this progressive fish project. She was a tough little trooper, though, and she hung right in there.

In those days, everything was fried in lard, so Mom got out the big iron frying pans and got the lard rolling hot. She rolled the fish in flour and dropped them in the hot lard. We thought those fish smelled fishy before, but when they hit that hot grease, it got really bad. Poor Mom couldn't take any more and she went out the back door. Every time she tried to come in, she would start gagging again. I can remember feeling so sorry for her as she stood outside on the back porch and gave orders to my older sister on how to finish preparing the meal. She finally came in and went into the far bedroom and closed the door. There she remained until we ate supper and opened the doors to rid the place of the fish smell.

None of us kids could eat any of the fish, so my sister had to fry eggs for us, but Dad would not give in and he did eat them.

From then on, when Dad wanted fish, Mother had to get everything else prepared and retreat into the closed bedroom while my oldest sister fried Dad some fish. When supper was over, all the kitchen doors were opened and when the smell was somewhat gone, Mother would come out.

The fish were thawing a little faster than Dad could eat them because he was receiving no help from anyone else, so he took them out in the front yard and buried them in a snowdrift to preserve them. When he wanted some, he would dig them out, take them in, and prepare them.

They were only buried a couple of nights when one morning, when we got up, it looked like all the dogs in the neighborhood had been in our front yard. They had fish and pieces of fish strung all over our front yard.

Dad was not too happy, but I am sure it was someone who was looking out for Mother that guided those dogs into the fish. Dad never ever brought up the incident again, nor did he ever order any more fish.

Winter Sickness

I can always relate winters to being sick. I can remember my aunt and neighbors referring to me as looking, "peak-ed." I always felt this indicated I resembled a runt in a litter of pigs.

During the winter months, we had virtually no fresh fruit or vegetables, so it is very likely we children were undernourished.

When we walked home from school we had to walk through the neighbor's barnyard, and many times the neighbor lady would call my brother and me in to have Ovaltine with their boys. Their boys were a year or two older and were big, strapping boys that made us look quite anemic.

The Ovaltine tasted delicious and I am sure the lady gave it to us because she felt we needed it very much.

Ovaltine was a hot cocoa type of drink supposedly full of all kinds of nutrients for growing children, but it was quite expensive, and prohibitive on the grocery list of our family.

It seemed like one of us six children was sick almost all winter. Colds were continuous. If there wasn't a cold in the family, one would be picked up at school and it would start a chain reaction. I could live with a cold, but we would get what everyone called the flu.

The flu came in different types. I usually got the kind that started with chills, fever, and ache all over. Some of my brothers and sisters would get chills, fever, and diarrhea.

As I was coming down with the flu, Mom would put me to bed on an old sofa in the room where the pot-bellied wood stove was located. Dad would fill the stove with wood until the sides became red and Mom would pile on the blankets. There I would lie shivering and shaking with the chills. In a couple of hours, I would become so hot I could hardly stand it, or I might become what they called "out of my head." If this happened, I would have a feeling of scary, cloud-like formations floating through my head and body. It was a terrible, scary feeling and I fought to keep my eyes open because it became worse when I closed them. This feeling would eventually overpower me sometime during the night, and I might awaken in another part of the house because "you were walking around out of your head." Sometimes I would awaken because Mom was sitting beside me putting cold compresses on my forehead. I fought to stay awake and hoped daylight would hurry and come so maybe the terrible scenes would go away.

Mom always left a kerosene lamp burning in the room with us, but the dancing shadows from the erratic burning of the wick in the lamp only added to the horror of the feeling that encompassed our bodies.

All the next day I would be cold and hot as Mom tried to force me to eat or drink. It was dreadful to go into that second night because I knew what to expect.

Mother would again pile on the blankets that I demanded to try to get warm. Sometime toward morning of the second night, I would awaken to find myself and the bed clothing completely soaked from perspiration. The perspiration odor was unlike a working perspiration odor and Mom would always say, "Well, it smells like your fever broke."

I would now have lost the chills, fever, and terrible weird unstable feeling that enclosed my head and body. I would now feel very weak and every bone and muscle in my body would ache. Mom would make me get out of bed so she could change the bedding. I could hardly get up and sit in a chair because I was so weak. Mom would bring me hot chocolate, but I didn't want to do anything except sleep.

It was then an uphill battle to recover. I always ended with a chest inflammation and no appetite. Mom would cook or boil onions and strain off the juice or syrup from the onions. She would mix sugar with this and then I was supposed to take a couple of spoonfuls of this hot fluid. It was a hateful process and sometimes ended up with an up-chucking of all that went down.

After a couple of days of not eating and not having a bowel movement, it was decided that what I needed was a "dose of castor oil."

A dose of castor oil was a large spoonful and was the most awful tasting stuff ever concocted. All of us children went through the "dose of castor oil treatment" at some time or other.

When you had six children, they did not all have the same disposition. Some were a little more, as Dad would say, "bull-headed" than the others. So it was that if you didn't take your castor oil for Mom, you were threatened with, "I'll have Dad give it to you when he comes in from doing chores." We had all experienced Dad holding my brother down on the floor and him and Mom forcing the castor oil in his mouth. This was a shocking experience to us when we were younger, and we would hold out until we heard Dad coming into the house.

I can remember special occasions where Mom would have Dad pick up a few oranges when he did the shopping. She would then give you half an orange to eat if you took your castor oil. How good that orange tasted and how you dreamed that someday when you were rich you would buy all the oranges you could sit down and eat.

The castor oil treatment resulted in many experiences that should have discouraged Mother from ever using it again.

The flu left you weak and wobbly. All you felt like doing was staying in bed and sleeping. When you began to get stomach cramps and bowel movement symptoms from the castor oil, you put off getting up just as long as you possibly could. We only had the one white enamel pot in the house and that was religiously kept in Mom and Dad's bedroom. When the castor oil did its job, there were times you stalled a little too long, and being weak and slow anyway you just never made it to the pot in time. This resulted in soiled clothing or an occasional soiled bed. Fortunately, the floors were either linoleum or hard varnished wood that cleaned up easy. I can't even imagine a carpeted room anywhere between the old pot and our upstairs bedroom in those days.

The castor oil "cleaning out" treatment that at that time seemed to be a necessary requirement to get over the flu only made one weaker and, if anything, probably resulted in prolonging the recovery period.

It seemed every year a few of us were always home sick with the flu or some other sickness during the highlight of the winter—the Christmas school play celebration and the coming of Santa to the local town.

One winter at this critical time, we were hit with the chickenpox. I believe all six of us kids were at a different stage with the pox. The Santa in town visit was once a year time when we got our own bag of candy, and this was a time we really cherished.

On the Saturday of the big day, we all demanded we were better. I know I was broken out all over and I was itching unbearably. We all set up such a scene and carried on so that Mom and Dad had a big conference.

Santa came to our small town which was about two and one half miles away, but he was also in the neighboring, larger town which was about twelve miles away. Mom and Dad knew that everyone in the neighborhood knew we had chickenpox, and they also knew they would be the talk of the neighborhood if they were seen in town with the kids all plastered with chickenpox. So it was decided to bundle us all up real good and take us to the neighboring town. This was a larger town and hopefully no one would recognize us.

We got to the scene where Santa was to arrive and Dad parked as close as possible. Mom had found plenty of big clothing and big scarves. She had us well bundled and when we heard the sirens of the fire truck approaching, with Santa waving from on top, Mom used the big scarves to cover the faces of those that were most obviously displaying the pox. As soon as the fire truck stopped, we children all jumped out, and chickenpox was the furthest thing from our mind as we rushed to get in line for our free bag of candy. Mom and Dad remained out of sight in the car. When we were through the line, we rushed back to the car to deposit our bag of goodies and begged to go through the line again, but Mom and Dad hurried us in the car and we were soon on our way out of town.

It was a common practice for the older children to go through the free candy line more than once, so we felt somewhat slighted but still thankful we got to go at all.

We would many times break out in a slight rash or itch and for some unknown reason the words "seven year itch" were applied as a diagnosis of what we had. Usually a good bath and a little rubbing alcohol took care of the problem.

There was one winter to remember when we broke out more severe than normal. I think all of us kids had broken out and it was miserable because our entire body was covered with an itching rash. This spread through school like wildfire and the words "seven year itch" had us scared real bad. We felt there was no way we could go on living for seven years with this miserable malady.

The mothers got together on the party line and somebody came up with a treatment for this itch that consisted of a concoction of sulfur and lard. This was mixed together into a paste and rubbed over your entire body. You then had to wear your complete bodysuit long underwear all the time to prevent this stuff from soiling your clothing and bed coverings. You can imagine the odor and discomfort this made when applied over one's entire body.

This itch did not affect anyone other than to make them miserable, so there was a neighborhood agreement that the children could continue to go to school. I am sure the teacher would have liked to have had some input into that decision.

Fortunately, this itch did not last seven years, but it did last a long time, and whether it just ran its course or the sulfur and lard cured it I guess will always remain a mystery.

SATURDAY 4

Gathering Eggs

Mondays were always dreary on the farm because boyhood weeks were measured from Saturday to Saturday. This was because Saturday was the most important day of the week. It was the day field work was cut short, chores were started early, and you went to town to do the trading.

It was not called shopping at that time. I suppose it was called trading because that is what took place. You took the eggs in and traded them for groceries and hoped you had enough eggs to cover the cost of the weekly groceries.

When I became old enough to relieve my older brother or sister of another duty, I was assigned to collect the eggs each day. If any were exceptionally dirty, I was supposed to wash them before they were put into the egg crate.

I always reserved the opinion that chickens had to be the dumbest things on the farm. They had plenty of nice clean nests to lay their eggs in, but many were too dumb to use the nest.

In the chicken house, Dad had erected poles for the chickens to roost on at night. I didn't know why at the time, but chickens just don't sleep on the ground. They must get up off the ground on a perch and that's where they sleep. This is called roosting.

While they sleep, their digestive track continues to work, so a platform is built under the roosting poles to catch the droppings they deposit at night. Some of these chickens, dumber than the others, always had a habit of laying their eggs on this platform full of chicken droppings. An old rake was kept leaning against the door frame, and every day I had to rake a few eggs off this dropping platform. By the time I raked them over close enough to pick them up, I really didn't want to even touch them. These eggs made up the majority of eggs I was supposed to wash after every gathering.

The big crates held thirty dozen eggs. The eggs fit into the crates in layers. Each layer was divided by cardboard dividers and each divider folded up for storage, but when opened, it formed thirty-six separate compartments, one for each egg. The layers were stacked five to each side of the crate.

I was never too keen on washing eggs, so if I could sneak it, I would hide the dirty eggs in the bottom of the crate and make sure the top rows were nice and clean.

When we took our eggs to the market, they did not take them out and look them over. We just gave them our full crate and they gave us an empty replacement.

When the chickens were producing good, we would always have a thirty-dozen case full. When they were doing real well, we had a small fifteen-dozen case we would put the extras in. Mom always wanted the cases to come out to an even dozen, so sometimes I would have to go looking for hidden nests to fill out the crate. Once in a while this would result in finding a hen that had gone into the hay mow or into a corner of grass somewhere and hidden a nest. The hen would deposit an egg a day until she had twelve or fifteen eggs in the nest; then she would set on the nest and hatch the eggs. Dad did not like to have chickens of all sizes running around the farm, so he would buy his chickens in the spring and try to prevent individual hens from hatching their own clutches.

So it was that whenever we found a hen on a nest, we took the eggs. These eggs, after having been set on by the hen, always took on a different look than a fresh egg. The shells were always a putrid-looking gray color and shiny like glass. Some probably had half-developed embryos in them and those that were not fertile would have spoiled inside.

These eggs were gathered and also hidden in the far bottom layers of the crates.

It always kind of amused me to wonder what really happened to these eggs when they reached their destination of usage.

This was taking place back in the thirties when money was scarce, so I am sure all the farmers did the same. This was probably what eventually brought about what was called "candling of eggs."

Candling got its name from the egg buyer holding the egg in front of a candle and looking through it to see if it was fresh. Our buyer began doing this, but used a small electric bulb. This ended our robbing of setting hen nests and selling all the eggs we could find.

This opened up an all new fun thing. When we could no longer put the stolen nest eggs in the crate, we would try to plan all kinds of things to do with them.

It was fun to throw them and see them explode against anything we hit. We sometimes took them into the pig yard and bombed the pigs. The pigs did not mind because they would eat every last drop they could find. It was fun to splat one up against a big fat pig and watch the other fight to lick it off. The eggs that were really rotten would explode with a loud pop, and soon the foul smell would bring all the pigs running.

The Tavern

Saturday night in town was the biggie of the week. Chores had to be done early so you could get to town and get your parking place. If you got to town early enough, you always got the same parking place right in front of the busy grocery store.

The town only had a population of four hundred and supported two grocery stores. My dad and uncle always parked side by side and cursed on anyone that might beat them to their parking places.

Dad would carry the eggs into the back of the store and go to the tavern to play euchre. Mother would do the shopping and the groceries were put in the empty egg cases. At that time there were no deep freezers, so nothing was frozen. The crate of paid for groceries were left sitting in the store, and when Dad was through playing cards, he would carry them out and place them in the car. The thought of someone stealing something from your crate of groceries never happened and never entered anyone's mind.

When Mom was through shopping, she joined two of my aunts in one of the cars. There they spent the night talking about everyone that walked by and all the gossip of the week.

If the card game lasted a little longer than usual, Mom would send my brother and me down to the tavern to tell Dad she was ready to go home. It would have been a terrible disgrace for a woman to have been seen in a tavern at that time. It was simply unheard of.

Nor were children seen in the tavern even if their Father was present with them. Maybe this is why my brother and I liked to take messages to Dad in the tavern. Sometimes we could linger awhile and hear conversations and words like we never heard anywhere else.

The tavern was always very dark and smoky. The odor of beer and bodies met you at the entrance. The ceilings were high and dirty, and usually one electric cord hung down over each card table. This cord had a small light bulb and shade on the end.

There were a few spittoons around, but not ample enough to serve the needs. If the spittoons were handy, the spitter aimed in that direction and hoped for the best, but if nothing was handy, it was left to fly in whatever direction was handy. Nothing could really damage the old plank flooring that probably got swept once a week, if it were lucky.

I remember one real old neighbor was playing cards at the same table as Dad. He was white haired, skinny, and badly wrinkled. My brother and I were standing by the table watching when this old fellow began to cough. He coughed real hard, then spit a big slug out on the floor. It landed fairly close to us because we talked afterward about seeing blood in it. This was scary to us and we talked about it that night in bed. We were sure the old fellow would be dead by morning. We talked of this many times after that, probably because the old fellow lived for many years and we could not quite understand how he kept going.

If we thought no one was watching us in the tavern, we would sneak a glance at the picture on the calendar. It was a picture of a pretty lady walking her dog. The dog was on a leash and had gone between her legs. Between the dog and the

Author in wagon with puppy

wind, it had her skirt up high enough so both of her upper thighs were visible.

One time our attention was centered on an individual in the tavern who was more boisterous than anyone else. Dad hurried us out with a message that he would be out as soon as he finished his game. We took our time and later heard Dad telling Mom about so and so getting real drunk that night. We were fascinated to think we might have witnessed a real live drunk.

Outdoor Movies

When the weather became warm and the ground dry, the free movies would start. This happened because people were beginning to get more mobile and cars became more plentiful. The small towns were losing some business to larger towns. If someone heard about eggs selling for a penny a dozen more in a neighboring town, they would go there to do their shopping. This inspired the local merchants to go together and sponsor a free movie. All it amounted to was a man with a projector and screen. He would set up on a vacant lot near the business district.

We kids always had to get there early to get a good seat. There was room for everyone, but as kids, we had a difficult time waiting. Anyway, this gave us a chance to tease the girls. Everyone except the grownups sat on the ground. The grownups brought folding chairs and boxes to sit on. The girls sat in the front, the boys next, and the grownups in the back. Because the girls were in front of us, it was easy to torment them. We would throw wads of grass at them, pull their hair, and steal anything we could get away from them. They would pretend like they were really upset, but I am sure they loved every minute of it. Anyway, it was a good way to pass the time until it was dark enough for the movie to show up good on the screen.

Once in a while we would get rained out in the middle of a cowboy and Indian fight. If it were a fast rainstorm and passed over, the operator would set up again and continue. If not, we would go home disappointed, wondering who won the battle.

The projector was the type that when one reel ran out, everything was stopped while the reel was rewound. The continuation of the movie was then put in, another reel threaded through, and the movie continued. This always gave us time to start another fight with the girls or to run over behind the old abandoned ice house and take a pee.

When the movie was over, Dad would go into the grocery store and pick up the crate of groceries Mother had bought. The crate fit nicely on the floor in the back seat of Dad's 1929 Chevrolet. It did not leave much room for three or four of us kids, but we did not squabble because we were quite sure we would get our usual ice cream cone now. This was routine, but always quite a decision over which flavor to choose. They had only chocolate, strawberry, and vanilla, but it was still a big decision. This was shortly confused more with the addition of butter pecan and maple nut. Eventually raspberry ripple was introduced, and I no longer had a problem with my choice, for that was my flavor forever.

As we grew to know the town better, we looked for more exciting things to do. Girls were always plentiful, but we were not yet at the age where they interested us enough to divert us from other experiences.

Spending Our Allowance

We always stayed close to Mom until she got her Saturday night shopping done. If she had a little money left, she would give each of us a few pennies, and on rare occasions, a nickel. We would then take off to meet our cousin and the neighbor boys. We would walk the street wondering what to spend our money on.

It was always a toss-up which store to spend our money in. One grocery store was eliminated entirely from our choice of spending our pennies because it weighed out every piece of bulk candy, if that is what we desired to buy.

The other grocery store was our choice if we could get the clerk we wanted. The owner was very conservative and carefully weighed out the candy, but if his helper was at the candy counter, he just heaped the bag full and never weighed it. He always heaped the bag full regardless of if we bought three cents worth or a nickel's worth. We got smart. If we were fortunate enough to get a nickel, we would get Mom or Dad to give us five pennies and always asked for three cents worth of candy and then use the other two cents for something in the drugstore.

Whenever we decided to spend our money in the good candy grocery store, it was always for chocolate covered peanuts, caramels, or plain chocolate stars.

We would always wait outside the store and watch for some-one to get the liberal clerk at the candy counter. When this hap-pened, we would give the others the sign and everyone rushed in and bought before he left the counter.

As we got older, other interests crept into our Saturday night activities. Two of the boys in the gang decided they were ciga-rette smokers. We had all tried corn cob pipes and corn silk, but now we were getting older and thought cigarettes were a great deal more sophisticated. Their Dad rolled his own cigarettes, but he would buy an occasional pack of tailor-mades and these boys would steal one or two out of the pack during the week. They would save them until Saturday night when we would all go down the alley between Turner's Grocery and Tom's Barber Shop, and there we would light them up and pass them around. We felt this was really getting us into the big time now. I can remember how terrible the first mouthful of smoke tasted. Every-body would watch everybody else to see if they inhaled the smoke. The best we non-inhalers could do was to hold the smoke in our mouth as long as possible and pretend we inhaled before easing it out. The two that furnished the cigarettes must have been making smoking a regular practice because it wasn't long before they were really inhaling. They would then watch the others of us and make sure we tried.

I can remember the first time I tried; I choked and coughed until my eyes watered. I just thought I must have done some-thing wrong and would not ever try that again.

While walking the streets, one of the smokers noticed some-one flip away a good sized live cigarette butt. This was too great a temptation for one of our smokers, so he called a conference behind the corner of Hill's Drugstore.

He said, "I got a plan to get that butt. We will all just walk along the street and when we get near the butt, one of you guys give me a shove toward it."

Everything went well and when we got near the burning butt, we pretended like we had a little scuffle and somebody gave him a shove. He faked a fall beside the butt and when he got up, he had it in his hand. Down the alley we went and passed it all around.

Thus, picking up live butts became quite a practice, and we soon pegged the smokers who threw away the big butts. We zeroed in on them. I am surprised we didn't get reprimanded, for it must have been very obvious what we were doing.

This picking butts continued but it did not completely fulfill the pretended smoking needs, so one Saturday night when we grouped, one of the smokers said, "I can get a pack of Marvels for twelve cents; let's see how much money we got altogether."

The five of us pooled our money and we were two cents short. Then one said, "Oh, I can get that from Dad," and he took off.

It was only a short while and he was back with the necessary two cents.

The oldest of the group was my cousin and he was 12, so he was designated to go buy the cigarettes. His folks were very close friends of the store owner we were going to buy from, so he used that as an excuse not to be able to do the job. It finally came down to the oldest of the smokers who was the main pusher of this smoking operation.

He took off and it wasn't long before he was back with our first pack of real cigarettes. We each got an entire cigarette apiece, and now we were really big time as we lit up. I still couldn't inhale, and by the time I finished just puffing that cigarette, I had a real good headache. I think my brother and cousin did, too, because later that night, when we got off alone, we decided it was a pretty dull night with a headache, our money gone, and no candy. The smokers kept the remaining cigarettes and were the only ones that really benefited from the entire operation.

From then on we spent our Saturday nights together by ourselves and stayed away from the costly cigarette smokers.

Turning to Crime

We became acquainted with a boy who lived in town and one night he suggested we go stealing grapes. He knew of someone in town that raised grapes and he knew just how to get into the patch. So away we went on a whole new venture.

We didn't have any grapes on our farm, and the only time I had ever eaten any was once or twice when we had gone to buy apples in the fall. Dad would buy a couple of bushels of apples and sometimes a small basket of grapes. I could vividly remember how good they were, so even though I was a little scared, I was anxious to get some grapes.

We sneaked through the alleys and finally got into the grape patch. They were suspended on trellises, so by getting down and looking up, you could see the bunches of grapes against the skyline. The only problem was that you could not see how ripe they were so you had to pick and eat, hoping you would get some ripe ones.

I am sure the man had picked all the ripe grapes because we never found any that were ripe, but we did eat a lot trying. My stomach was bothering some when I went to bed that night, but it was nothing compared to the next day.

After noting I was running to the toilet all morning, Mother finally wanted to know what was wrong. I told her I just had a little belly ache, but little did she know it was more than just a little.

That ended our grape stealing but it did prepare us for the strawberry stealing that was to follow the next summer.

The same boy introduced us to this venture and showed us a couple of patches. We didn't have strawberries on our farm, so they were another treat we were looking forward to.

We never had very good success stealing many because I am sure everyone kept them picked quite clean, and again, it was very difficult to tell the ripe from the green at night.

One night my cousin said he knew of a patch in town that we had never tried. The only problem was that the people who owned them were very good friends of his folks, and he was afraid if he ever got caught he would really be in deep trouble.

It just so happened we saw these friends all downtown visiting, so we decided this would be a good time to go hit their patch of berries.

My cousin hung back until my brother and I were in the patch, then he came in. We were going pretty good and even putting some in our pockets when a car pulled into the driveway. We didn't have a chance to run without being seen, so we all flattened ourselves down in the patch. We must have really got flat because it was the owner who drove in and he then flashed a spotlight all over the patch.

How I now longed to be someplace else and wondered why we chose to do such a foolish thing. I felt sure he could see us. I was waiting for him to yell, "Come out of there, you outlaws!"

I was wondering what we were going to say to him, and even more concerned about what we would say to our parents.

The light swished around for what seemed forever, then it all at once went out.

How could he ever have missed seeing us?

The car door slammed. I lay there buried in the patch trembling and promising anyone listening that if I were let go this time, I would never ever do this again.

Soon the house door slammed. Somebody said, "Let's get out of here!"

We exploded out of the berry patch and never stopped running until we were blocks away. We eased out under a street light to survey ourselves. I had on a light-colored short-sleeved shirt with a pocket in the front. I had been putting strawberries in this pocket when the owner turned on the light. Not having a chance to empty the pocket, I had lain flat on those strawberries and now had the pocket and part of my shirt completely stained, plus I smelled like a fresh dish of crushed strawberries. This now presented us with a problem almost as serious as being caught in the patch.

We decided we didn't have time to go to the park and wash the shirt and hope it would dry. Finally, my brother came up with the idea we should tell the folks that our cousin had poured strawberry pop in my pocket.

We sneaked into the car without being discovered, but when we got home, it couldn't be hidden any longer.

Mother said, "What in the world happened to your shirt?"

I told her the story that we were fooling around and my cousin poured my pocket full of strawberry pop.

Dad was in the barn checking the cattle at the time and Mom made me take the shirt off and give it to her for soaking. I am sure Dad never knew about the shirt. I don't believe Mom was fooled by the story. I think she had a good idea what happened, but she also knew that Dad would get the leather strap and work us over good if he thought we were in somebody's strawberry patch. Mom approved of disciplinary action, but I know it hurt her when Dad got a little too rough with us.

Mom's diplomacy worked because we felt we had been fortunate to get out of two close calls, so we vowed never to try stealing anything again.

SCHOOL⁵

Author is second from left, second row

Author is second from left, front row

Games and Things

Our country grade school was called Oak Grove and was located about a mile from our home. It was the typical, one room square building, located in the center of an acre of land. It was heated by an enormous wood furnace in the basement. There was one large register in the middle of the floor upstairs. In the winter this register was used for multiple purposes. Beside trying to heat the uninsulated high ceiling building, the furnace was used to dry wet clothing and to heat our lunches.

Some children had to wear the same clothes for school that they wore to the barn. When they got these clothes wet and crowded their clothes and themselves over the big, hot register, the schoolroom took on quite an offensive odor. I did prefer this odor over an occasional first or second grader who wet their pants, and was then set on or near the register to dry.

Our family was fortunate because we had a set of clothing for school and one for the barn, and it was best you were never caught wearing the wrong clothes in the wrong place.

In the early spring we would get to school before the teacher because we rode with Dad when he took the milk to the cheese factory. We could not get into the schoolhouse until the teacher came and unlocked the door.

One morning, as we all walked into school with the teacher, someone noticed a window open. A little closer look showed our big flag all crumpled up on a bench that was close to the window. The teacher immediately decided someone had opened the window, climbed in and, using the flag to cover up with, had spent the night in the schoolhouse.

This excited all of us and it was a big race to meet and tell all the other children as they arrived.

We had farther to walk home than most kids, and by the time we got home, the party line had it spread around the neighborhood that our school had been broken into over night and some things were missing. We felt quite proud to be able to set Mother straight with the proper story.

We had no playground equipment except a ball and bat, so we created our own games. We boys played a lot of cops and robbers. We would have a pretend bank and the robbers would come and hold it up. The chase was then on. The chase could only go one place and that was around and around the schoolhouse. We would then shoot at each other by throwing empty twelve-gauge shotgun shells at each other. If you got hit, you were supposed to drop. We found the empty shells would catch the air and would not fly very fast or straight, so we took two shells and jammed one tightly inside the other. This made a compact, heavier, projectile that threw much better. The problem was if you got hit in the head or face, the brass edges of the shell would make quite a bruise and sometimes even break the skin. This went on until someone went home with a pretty good cut or a contusion that looked like it was going to explode. Their Mother would call the teacher and our cops and robbers shell game would end for a while.

Somewhere in about the middle of my grade-school tenure, a truck pulled into the schoolyard one day and two men began to unload and set up a swing set. This set had three swings and a teetertotter. This was the greatest thing that ever hit our school.

Of course, I am sure it was a headache for the teacher because the larger children took over everything.

We had about a fifteen-minute recess in the morning and afternoon, and a half or three-quarters of an hour recess at noon. The teacher got smart and let the little youngsters out five or ten minutes ahead of the older students so they had the new equipment all to themselves for a short period of time.

This new equipment soon grew old and we boys were back to our old cops and robbers game.

The snow-thawing days of winter were always welcome because it meant snowball fights. Two forts were built and we chose up sides. All the older girls and boys participated. When we had a male teacher, he was out there in the middle of the fight with us. Occasionally, one of the girls would get a solid smack straight in the face that would send her to the schoolhouse with tears, but it usually wasn't long and she was right back out for more. When the bell rang for school, we would take our mittens and wring as much water out as possible, then put them on the big heat register to dry. Our pants were usually wet so we were allowed to take our workbooks and a chair and sit around the register to dry. The schoolroom did not need a humidifier.

Spring

After a long cold winter, the first warm days of spring were the most welcome time of the year. Those first few warm days, when you discovered a few blades of green grass along the south wall of the house, started the exasperating struggle with Mom to release us from the wearing of four buckle overshoes and heavy coats to school.

The ground was still like a wet sponge, and every time you fell down you had wet knees. The noon-hour recess at school ended in a disaster for many who took a few too many falls. With the warm sun glowing in the unshielded school windows and the furnace still full of hard oak coals from the morning fire, the schoolroom about this time of day was like an unvented oven.

Because the mothers communicated quite closely about changing to summer clothing, everyone was still wearing their winter clothes. This included the long underwear and heavy coats.

If you weren't wet from falling down, you were wet from perspiration.

I know that our family was as clean as many, and perhaps a little cleaner than some because we had a bath and clean underwear every Saturday night. Many of the kids were not that fortunate.

When you got a group like this gathered in a real hot room, you can imagine the odor that would begin to generate. In addition, some that got the wettest might be seated beside the register to dry out. This added to the stench.

If it got real bad, the teacher would open a window on each side of the room. I can vividly remember the welcome smell of that fresh spring air, and flowing in with it would be the joyous song of the meadowlark. The meadowlark always used the big white oak corner post below the schoolhouse for its pulpit. There it would rapturously announce to the entire world that spring had arrived.

We could walk along the county highway about halfway to school. It had a surface covering of what we called gravel, but what was later properly called crushed rock.

The two wheel tracks of vehicles were packed quite solid, so that is where we walked. Because of traffic, most of the time we could walk the entire one-half-mile distance of the road without ever getting off the tracks.

At this time of year, the shoulders of the road were a heavy, thick mud gumbo mixed with sparse amounts of crushed rock. We didn't like it when a car came along and forced us to walk along the side of the road in this sticky gumbo.

On one particular afternoon, as we walked home from school, we could hear a car coming. As it approached, we noted it was a Model T Ford and traveling very slow. We had to leave our solid, nice walking, and get off into the mud on the shoulder. This mud would fast accumulate on your boots until they were twice the normal size and very heavy. Everyone was sort of unhappy about this and was putting the blame of this inconvenience on the approaching Model T Ford.

One of the more daring of the group said, "Let's fix him when he goes past. Everybody load your boots up real full and when he goes past, stand close and let fly with a good hard kick."

I was the smallest and youngest of this group of five, and this sort of scared me, but I wanted to be one of the big guys so I got ready with the rest of them. As the old Ford went chugging slowly past, everybody let fly with a good hard kick. The mud, mixed with crushed rock, rattled against the side of the old Model T, creating streaks of big brown globs up and down the side of the car.

This wasn't bad enough. It so happened we recognized the driver of the car. He was a little different sort of individual. He was probably in his sixties and his complexion was quite dark. He had always lived alone, seldom cut his hair and his beard was long and gray. This was unusual in that time of short hair cuts and no beards. He was shorter than the average man and walked with a sort of shuffle. The only time we ever saw him was on the street in town, and we avoided him because he looked like the villain in one of the free movies we had seen.

So it wasn't bad enough that we kicked mud on this guy's car; one of the boys had to yell, "Take that ya black bastard."

After this explosive display, the little old Model T began to grind to a halt. Fortunately for us, the poor brake system gave us time to realize what was happening. Since I was the smallest and because my boots were still heavy with mud, I was the last one to reach the fence everyone was heading for. I could just see this vicious looking character catching me while the others made their escape into the nearby woods.

I did manage to roll under the fence where my brother grabbed me and helped me to my feet. He held my wrist and half dragged me into the heavy cover of the nearby woods. My heart was in my throat as one of the older boys stood behind a tree giving us a progress report. "He's coming up to the fence.

If he gets over the fence, we better start running again," he reported.

"He's standing by the fence now. Now he is yelling something but I can't understand what he is saying. Now he's shaking his fist this way. There he goes walking back to the car."

I was really relieved when I heard he was going back to the car. Soon we heard the old Ford start up and go on its way.

We waited a long time to see if he might come back, but eventually we felt it safe enough to venture out. Everyone laughed and tried to joke over the incident, but there was a definite cloud of, "maybe we went a little too far this time," hanging over the entire group.

The incident was almost forgotten until late Saturday afternoon when Dad returned from his trip to town. He came into the house carrying the thirty dozen egg crates filled with groceries, set them on the floor, and taking off his jacket, he went into the closet. In this closet, hanging on a special hook, was an old leather belt, better known as the strap. This belt had only one purpose in existence and that was to "keep you boys in line," as Dad put it.

When Dad came out of the closet, he had one hand behind his back, but the strap could be seen hanging down behind him. Looking at my brother and me he said, "I heard in town that you boys kicked mud all over black Bill's car the other day and called him an "old black bastard."

There wasn't much we could say. We knew we were now in as much trouble as we had probably ever been in in our entire life, and we were really going to get it. My brother did come up with, "We didn't call him any names."

Dad said, "But you did kick mud on his car when he went past?"

We never lied to Dad, so the best we could come up with was, "Well, everybody else did, too."

It was always best if you could get the first whipping because it was over fast and you did not have to watch the other guy get it while you painfully stood by waiting your turn.

Dad had a way with the strap that reflected his feelings. If he was quickly aroused by something we did wrong, his reactions were fast and furious, resulting in the strap getting to its mark in a more severe, accurate fashion. If it were something such as our car mud incident, where he had to penalize some time after the incident, his tactics were somewhat different. Maybe it was because he could see the fear in our faces as we hovered in the corner awaiting our fate. At any rate, he could make the strap sound like it was inflicting much more damage than it really created. Between the noise of the strap and the noise we made, it sounded like we were suffering greatly. Sometimes when it really got loud and our sisters began to cry from fear and compassion, Mother would say to Dad, "I think that is enough now; they learned their lesson."

We both ended up in the back room crying.

What probably hurt the most was that we were not on hand to watch Mom unpack the groceries.

The groceries were the only contact we had with the good things of the outside world during the wet and winter part of the year. It was at this time Dad had to either walk to town or take the team and wagon because the roads were not passable by car.

We always looked forward to the experience of watching Mom unpack the bags and boxes, and we would get as close as possible so we could get that special grocery-store smell from the boxes, bags, and contents.

We could always be assured the groceryman had stuffed a small bag of candy somewhere in the groceries. We could be just as assured it was not chocolate covered peanuts, caramels, or stars. It would be a bag of his slow moving hard candy. While we always waited for Mom to open the bag in hopes it was chocolates, we were happy with whatever fell forth.

On this day Mom finally said, "Well, you boys can come out now and share in the candy if you promise you won't pull a trick like that again." We had our feelings pretty well ripped apart and we didn't want to go out in front of our snickering sisters, so much as we hated to do it, one of us said, "We don't want any candy."

Mom had that built-in sense of knowing what our problem was, so she would give the girls their share of candy, then say, "All right, you girls get outside now; I got work to do."

The doors would slam and everything was quiet except for Mom busy in the kitchen.

We wondered, "Did she put the candy away?"

After a period of time, when she knew we were settled down and ready to come out, she would make it sound like she had something for us to do. She would say, "Come on boys, I'm just about out of kindling, you better get out and scare some up."

As we slowly scuffled out through the kitchen, she would reach over and stuff something in each of our pockets. We pretended like we could care less, but we could hardly wait to get out back of the woodshed where we could hurriedly check our pockets.

The Outdoor Toilets

Our one-acre schoolyard had a girl's outdoor toilet on the far northwest corner of the lot, and one for the boys on the far northeast corner. By the time school was over in the spring, there was a well-worn path to each toilet and the odor was present long before you reached the toilet.

During the winter, a trip to the toilet was a cold, miserable occasion that you put off as long as possible. The only good part about it was the nice, soft toilet tissue. At home all we had was the Sears and Montgomery Ward catalogs. You soon learned to choose the light gray sheets of the catalog and crumple them good first. This softened them and made them far superior to the slick colored sheets.

When school started you changed your toilet habits to fit the school program and the soft toilet tissue. Anyway, why waste good valuable play time at home when you could get the job done on school time?

During the first warm days of spring, I always worked in a few extra trips to the toilet. Many of these trips were not necessary, but it was so nice to get outside and hear and feel spring. I would usually slip around behind the toilet and pee up against the side of the toilet because it was nice to be outside, and it didn't stink nearly as bad as it did inside the toilet. Here I was hidden from view and could sort of daydream out across the far expanse of rolling hills.

There were two huge pine trees located on the back fence line of the school property and near the girl's toilet. These trees represented the means of separating the big boys from the little boys. This was done because only when you were big enough could you jump up and catch the lowest limb and pull yourself up in the tree.

The tree was then easy to climb, so we would climb high enough to look over the barricade in front of the door of the girl's toilet, and actually see the girls go in and out of their toilet. It really made you feel like one of the big guys when you made your first trip up, and sometimes you could create a little added zest to the conversation by using language that you could not use around the little kids on the ground.

There was always a great deal of commotion generated when one girl opened the toilet door and another might be exposed to our view as she sat on the hole opposite the door. One of us would let go with, "I seen London! I seen France! I seen Mary's underpants!"

"We're going to tell the teacher on you guys!" could be heard coming out of the crowded toilet.

Eventually all the girls would come boiling out of the toilet and race toward the school as we would yell, "We saw Mary, sitting on the hole, we saw Mary, sitting on the hole!"

A couple of these up-risings would soon bring an administrative directive from the teacher that would put the big trees off limits to climbing by the boys.

Sometimes we would go down to the crushed rock driveway and load our pockets with rocks. When the girls went into the toilet, we would bombard the toilet with rocks. This was also always good for a lot of screaming, but was again short-lived by a fast reprimand from the teacher.

Although the girls made it sound like they hated us for our little extra activities, I am sure the majority enjoyed it because it would only be a day or two later, and when the opportunity presented itself, one of the bold ones would volunteer a confession of who told the teacher. This girl was then labeled, "tattle-tail, tattle-tail."

She would usually respond with, "Liar, liar, pants on fire, nose as long as a telephone wire."

Fortunately for kids, they would soon forget differences, and new games and adventures were soon shared once again.

School Lunches

On our walks along the county highway to and from school, we kept a sharp surveillance for discarded decorative half-pint empty whiskey bottles. We always collected a few for our winter use. The bottles were taken home where they were washed, and when the weather became cold, we would carry hot chocolate to school in these bottles. About ten in the morning, the bottles full of hot chocolate were set on the big register in the floor and by noon, the contents were hot. Sometimes they were so hot we had to set them in the snow to cool before we could drink the contents. This fast change of temperatures would sometimes break the bottle, and this meant the loss of part of our noon meal. If you only had sorghum sandwiches for lunch, they just didn't slide down too well without the hot chocolate to help.

The big single register was located in the front center of the room, so you had to cross it when you approached the front of the room. We sat in seats in the back of the room and when a class was called, the children got up and went to the front of the school where they sat in chairs to attend their classes.

Periodically, someone would walk toward the front of the room, forgetting all about the bottles on the register, and they would walk right into them. There would be a tremendous crash as a cloud of stinky vapor and smoke would erupt as the spilled fluids hit the hot furnace below. Everyone scrambled to try to salvage their bottle. It was always a great disappointment when you found your bottle broken or spilled, completely empty.

Many of the bottles at that time were sealed with cork stoppers. Once in a while, someone would forget to loosen the stopper when they set their bottle on the register. As the contents heated, the pressure built up until all at once, "Ker-wham," would go the cork. It would usually fly up and hit the ceiling with a smack. This was amusing to the older kids and scared the daylights out of the younger ones.

If the cork was fitted too tight into the bottle so that it would not release, the bottle would then break. This usually broke up the learning routine of the school, and besides causing some excitement from the noise and stench, it interrupted and delayed the school monotony for a short while.

Some of us seventh and eighth grade boys predetermined that if we loosened the corks just slightly, the pressure would not break the bottle, but we could enjoy the excitement of a loud pop off. After a couple days of the same bottles popping off, and seeing the enjoyment we were experiencing, the teacher caught on and a little, "You aren't fooling me lecture," followed.

The big old wood furnace in the school basement not only heated our bottles of cocoa on its register, it also toasted our sandwiches.

We boys would go into the basement and open the door on the furnace. If we had something to hold our sandwiches with, we would then hold them over the coals until the bread toasted. This added greatly to an otherwise tasteless homemade headcheese sandwich.

If you were not fortunate enough to have a forked stick or piece of wire to run through your sandwich and hold it over the coals, you then just blew the dirt and ashes off the platform behind the big iron furnace door and laid your sandwich on there. Your sandwich would not get toasted, but by turning it quite often, it would get warm. Occasionally, a sandwich would slip off the forked stick or wire and fall into the fire. This was a sad day for the party it happened to because it might have been all he had to eat. Many times, the apple or piece of cake was eaten during a recess so all you had at noon was a sandwich. Usually when this happened, the others of us would break him off a bite from our sandwich and help him through his disaster.

Sometimes there was some food trading done. We always had homemade bread and after it was a few days old, it was dry and getting stiff. Occasionally, one family of three boys would have sandwiches made from boughten bread. Boughten bread was bakery bread bought at a store and seldom seen in school lunches. When these other boys would come with sandwiches made of boughten meat and bread, we would trade almost anything we had to try to get a bite of their sandwich. Occasionally, we would trade a piece of cake or an apple for half of one of their sandwiches. We ate it in nibbles to make it last because it was so good. We always thought if we just had boughten bread and butter for sandwiches, we wouldn't need anything else; but we were never that fortunate.

The Slow Learners

Our school attendance of fifteen to twenty students included a girl who was mentally retarded and a boy who was an epileptic. They both moved into our neighborhood when I was in the fourth grade. The girl was older than me and the boy younger. The girl was abnormal, so we all knew something was wrong with her, and after a few days, it was accepted and of no great concern.

The boy, except for a slight limp and slight speech impediment, looked normal, so he was accepted with those of his age.

The boy was seated directly across from me and although we had heard folks talk about him being an epileptic, we had no idea what it was until one day when he had a seizure. He was in his seat the same as always, when all at once he began to tremble and gurgle. His uncontrollable gyrations carried him out of his seat onto the floor beside me. His sister knelt beside him calling his name, but the pupils of his eyes were hardly visible and he transmitted no response above a gurgle. The front of his pants began to get all wet and this scared some of the girls and they began to cry.

I had experienced animals dying because I had been hunting with my dad and watched squirrels and rabbits die after he had shot them. I had also watched Dad butcher pigs on the farm and had watched them die. I was now sure this boy was dying because he was having all the same symptoms of all these animals I had watched die.

We did not have a telephone at the school, so the teacher stood by as helpless as everyone else.

After what seemed an eternal amount of time, the boy gradually settled down and soon regained his composure.

After this first seizure, others were accepted, but it was always scary to everyone and I was sure he was going to die each time he had one.

There were times the boy would not recover very soon, so the teacher would send one of the older children down to the cheese factory for help. The factory was about half a mile away, but was the closest source of communication and help. The boy's parents did not have a telephone, so the factory owner would drive over to their farm and tell them their boy was sick. Many times the boy's parents did not have a car that would run, so the factory owner would bring the mother to school and they would take the boy home.

I always had a sympathetic feeling for the little guy, and perhaps the teacher sensed this because I was eventually seated with him in a double seat and helped him with his school work.

I accepted this okay, but there were times the odor from him wetting his pants was almost unbearable. I never said anything to anyone about it because I was well aware of his condition and knew he could not help it.

Both of these children were given the same attention as other students, although their assignments were geared to their capability and other older students helped them. They played the same games and were included in all the outside activities that we participated in. They were always chosen last when we chose up sides to play ball or pump-pump-pull-away, but they were included and did their best to please us.

Author and brother Bud with ducks they raised

I was in my first year of high school when the boy got a bad seizure. His folks had no money or means to get him to a hospital, so he died at home. My brother and I were asked to be pallbearers. We were kind of apprehensive because we had never seen a dead person, let alone carry one. It was a new experience and many, many thoughts clouded my mind as we walked the casket toward the grave. The family was very sad because this was the only boy in a family of five children. I tried to keep one thing foremost in my thoughts, and it was that this boy was now at ease and would not have to suffer the humiliation of any more of those terrible seizures. It helped me get the job done.

The Balloon Incident

When the weather began to break in the spring, we would get a ride to school every other day with Dad when he took the milk to the cheese factory. We could only do this when the weather was warm enough for us to play outside because we could get to school before the teacher. There were usually many others who did the same, so we always had a game going when the teacher arrived.

One morning, when we had a frost the night before, we could see car tracks in the frosty grass that went behind the schoolhouse. We all followed them back there wondering if there was still a car back there. Seeing no car, we dismissed the issue until one boy came running and yelling that he had found a balloon back where the car had been parked. I was only in second grade at the time, but I can remember it being a sort of odd-looking balloon because it was the same diameter for its full length and had a big, wide opening. This didn't seem to bother anyone, and it was only a short time before the boy blew it up and we tied the end shut.

We were having a great time batting our new balloon around the school yard when the teacher drove in.

We had a man teacher that excelled in doing his job and getting along with us kids, but this time we could not understand his actions. Upon seeing our balloon, he got a very disgusted look on his face, and without any explanation of any kind, he seized the balloon and went straight down into the basement to the furnace. We were all appalled with his actions because all he said was, "That is not a balloon and you kids should never touch another if you ever see one."

We knew, from the tone of his voice, that we dare not pursue the balloon issue any more, and even though the mystery remained with us for a long time, we were soon to replace it this day with other interests.

Glorying in Attention

When I reached the eighth grade, I was the only one in that grade in our school and consequently, the oldest and biggest boy in school. I enjoyed an entire year of being looked up to and having a feeling of impressive importance.

The two seventh grade girls had a continuous rivalry going over seeing which one could command the most of my attention. I don't remember ever singling out one over the other, but I do remember liking them both and glorying in a year of flattery.

I liked the attention, but lacked the knowledge or aggressiveness to do any more than try to impress these girls by hitting the ball the farthest or running the fastest.

I do remember being sent down to the basement alone with one of these girls to study and learn parts of a Christmas play. She put a board on a block of wood and wanted me to sit there beside her. No way was I going to get that close. I wanted to in the deepest emotional way, but I just didn't have the nerve to follow through. I got my own block of wood and sat what I considered a safe distance away. I fantasized about that incident for the next two weeks, but had the same thing taken place again, I am sure the outcome would have been repeated. It did give me many tingling good feelings that I carried to bed with me many nights.

The Skunk

One early spring day, as we were walking home from school, someone spotted a skunk out in an open field. Someone else mentioned that skunk skins were worth a lot of money. My brother and I knew our dad had trapped and sold a few skunk pelts, so we could verify this statement. This was enough to encourage this hoard of monsters to grab sticks and rocks and descend down upon this skunk.

Since a skunk is a slow mover, it was easy to catch up to it and then the battle engaged.

The skunk was using his defense to his utmost ability but we all stayed far enough away so he did not get a direct hit. Granted, some of us were getting the results of the skunk's outside range, but after the first initial blast of smell, we were so involved in the kill that we ignored the smell.

With seven determined boys carrying on the battle, the skunk hardly had a chance, and eventually someone got in a lucky blow to the skunk's head. This was followed by closer and more accurate blows, and soon the skunk succumbed to the pressure.

The entire area surrounding the battle ground was polluted with skunk scent and, of course, we had all been running around in it so we were all well stunk-up.

We stood around our skunk like a bunch of starving natives around an elephant kill. We quoted big figures like, "I heard a good skunk hide is worth four dollars and fifty cents."

"Gee," somebody said, "That's over fifty cents apiece."

Another who thought he was a fur expert would say, "Yeah, but that's for the blacks; this one's got a big white stripe; he ain't worth as much."

When the excitement of the kill had subsided, the question of, "What do we do with it now?" came up.

We knew the only thing of value was the pelt, but none of us knew how to skin a skunk. Another knowledgeable character in the group came up with, "Boy, you got to be careful. My dad said he heard of somebody skinning one and they cut the piss bag and he stunk so bad they had to bury it under the straw pile." It was finally decided we would have to get one of the dads to skin our kill.

It seemed the enthusiastic interest began to dwindle a little as one boy said, "My dad has never skinned one. He wouldn't know how." Another followed with the same remark. This left my brother and me and my cousin. My cousin was older than either of us, and I am sure somewhat wiser, because it wasn't long before he talked us into taking it home with us because he was sure his dad was too busy to skin it.

A couple of the bigger boys went down to a nearby fence and broke off a piece of wire. We got a sturdy stick and through some trial and error, we finally managed to get that skunk hung on the stick so with one person on each end of the stick we could carry it quite conveniently.

As usual, Jimmy, our faithful dog, was waiting for us by the line fence gate. He could smell us before he could see us and as we approached, his hair stood up around the scruff of his neck and he growled as he backed away from us.

Jimmy kept his distance all the way home and I am sure he had a problem wondering why we chose to associate so close to this stinky critter.

We carried the skunk right up into the front yard and as we burst enthusiastically into the house, we were met with, "Phew, you boys get right out of this house as fast as you can!"

We stood out in the front yard by our kill that was now fast losing its popularity, while Mom did some questioning. When she was done she said, "Get that thing out behind the barn. I'll leave some clothes here on the sidewalk for you to change into and you take what you got on and hang them on the clothesline."

Mother was not very happy, but years later when I thought about this, I wondered if she didn't go into the house and shake her head while grinning and thinking "Why couldn't they have all been girls?"

By now, we were getting a little disappointed because we were not receiving the hero's welcome we had anticipated. Dad was still working in the field and we felt sure when he came in things would change.

When we saw him coming, we ran to meet him just bursting to ask him, "How much are skunk hides worth now?"

Our ego trip ended when Dad said, "This time of year they aren't worth anything. It is only in the fall when the skins are prime that they are worth anything."

By now his nose and knowledge of boys had told him why we had asked this question. "Boys," he said, "I think it best you take that skunk and go down in the night pasture, as far as you can go, and bury it deep enough to get rid of the smell around here."

Author with puppy

The only real satisfaction we got out of our skunk episode was that when we sat down at the supper table that night, our sisters got up and left. They took their meals into the living room and kept up a continuous muttering about how bad we smelled. Anything we could do to infuriate our sisters we considered a positive accomplishment, so we felt the skunk incident was not all lost in vain.

Getting All the Attention

Walking to and from school was a new experience each day. Four families of us walked about one half a mile together. In this group were seven boys. It was always a challenge to see who could spot the bottles in the ditch first. If it were an old bottle and no one wanted it, we would load up with rocks and on signal, everyone would start throwing to see who could break the bottle. If we found a fresh liquor bottle, the stopper was pulled and it was passed around for everyone to have a smell.

On one occasion, someone found a bottle that had quite a few drops remaining in the bottom. We had one boy in the group who was always more daring than any of the others, so he took the bottle, tipped it up, and drained the remaining contents into his mouth. He choked a little and his eyes watered as he tried not to show the shock and surprise he got from the strong contents. As he recovered his composure, he tried to impress all of us with his accomplishment. He changed his vocabulary to a great many words we were all forbidden to use. This made him the center of attention, as now he found he was entertaining all of us. At the time, we really did think he was slightly intoxicated and, of course, this helped him to think so also.

Before he departed down his lane that took him home and separated him from us, he was even walking a little erratic. We laughed and joked about him the remainder of the distance home.

The next day he was the center of attention. Everyone began questioning him about anything they had ever heard about someone who had been intoxicated. Some asked if he had a headache. Others asked if his folks had noticed anything wrong.

This boy was a good actor, especially when the older girls heard about it and began gathering around. He made the incident gather exciting momentum as it was repeated over and over. The contents in the bottle had grown from "the hell, it was only a few drops," to "the whole damn bottom was covered."

I cannot remember any other event that ever brought out the swear words seemingly necessary to express the details of this incident. The girls seemed to delight in hearing all this and kept asking questions that stimulated more exaggerated details. This incident was the talk of the school for almost a week before it finally died out.

Helping Teacher

Behind the school was located a big iron pump. A can hung on a hook on the pump and that's where we got our drinking water. The big kids had to pump for the little ones, but this never seemed to present a problem.

Sometimes one of us boys would hold our hands over the spigot where the water came out while one of the others pumped. The water would build up inside the pump and if you could hold it back, it would eventually run out the top of the pump. This created quite a head of pressure on your hand and if a girl was standing nearby, you just opened a small crack in your hand in her direction, and a spray of water would go ripping out, giving her a surprised soaking. This usually resulted in, "I'm going to tell the teacher on you."

Most of the time they never told on us.

The oldest boys were given their assignments each week, and one was to keep the galvanized water pail in the schoolhouse full of water. There was a long-handled dipper in the pail and everyone helped themselves when they wanted a drink.

Eventually, someone decided this was not the most sanitary thing in the world, so they purchased a big earthen crock with a lid and a spigot. This large crock was filled each day. Paper cups came with it and you took a paper cup, held it under the spigot, got your drink, and discarded the paper cup. This was such a novelty that the paper cups were soon all used up.

They were replaced with a single glass cup and things were back to the same sanitary situation as the pail and dipper.

It was the older boys' job to keep the water cooler filled and in the winter to keep the big furnace full of wood.

When I was the only eighth grader, I had these jobs alone. It made me feel impressive to handle these jobs, especially when I could lift a pail of water and dump it in the cooler while all the girls watched.

On Friday afternoon, during the last recess, sweeping compound was scattered on the hard wooden floor. This sweeping compound appeared to be sawdust soaked in some kind of good smelling oil. The little kids would run and slide on the compound. Every once in a while one would slip down and go scooting along on their rear down the aisle between the seats. This worked the oil from the compound into the floor. After school I would help sweep and pick up the compound. It was usually used several times before being discarded. At the end of every week, the teacher would give me a candy bar for my week of many chores.

This was a great treat because I had never had a candy bar all of my very own. Dad would play euchre on Saturday in the tavern in town and when he won, he would get nickel chips that were good for trade for anything at the bar. Dad did not drink, so he would take his trade in candy bars. When we children became restless during the week, Mother would pop up with one of these candy bars and it was cut up and divided among us. A candy bar shared four to six ways resulted in quite a small piece for each, so we invariably discussed how, "When I grow up I am going to buy a candy bar all of my own."

So after school, when I was real hungry, this candy bar was a real treat. The teacher usually gave me a Milky Way bar. I never ate it immediately. I waited until I was around the corner and out of sight of the schoolhouse on the way home. I would then slowly nibble off the soft bottom part and save the caramel part for last.

If a car came along, I would hide what I had left. It was usually someone from the area and they would offer me a ride, which I always accepted. It was a good feeling to get a ride part of the way home, especially when you had half of a candy bar in your pocket when you got out of the car.

Nothing equaled the taste of the caramel of that candy bar, and I prolonged its existence as long as possible.

I didn't tell anyone about my candy bar paycheck at the end of each week. I had somewhat of a deep feeling that if I told I would then have a guilt feeling of not sharing with them, but as long as it was my own secret, I felt no guilt.

When I was finished eating the bar, I would hide the wrapper down a gopher hole and cover it with dirt so the secret would not get out.

Author and relatives in background

RELATIVES

6

Author and family before last sister, Shirley, was born

Our Lazy Uncle

We were never too happy when one certain uncle and his family came out to visit and stay. It was my mother's sister and her family. Her husband was a cross country semi-truck driver.

My dad was a believer that if you were an able-bodied person who ate and slept at his house, other than on Sunday, you also helped with the farm work. If any of my other uncles were staying to visit, they would put on some old clothes and help with the farm work wherever they could, but not the uncle semi driver. He would eat and then move as far as the old couch on our screened-in porch, and there he would sleep.

He always looked like he hadn't had any sleep for days because his eyes were always red and had big bags under them. There were no sleepers on the trucks in those days, and he always talked of how he had been in California a few days before they came to our place. We always thought he drove for many hours to get back and out to our place so he could sleep for several days.

One time one of us kids noticed the sole on the shoe on his right foot. There was a round spot worn part way through the leather on the sole. We found out it was from the gas accelerator in the truck. At that time, all vehicles had a small, round metal foot pedal for an accelerator. They proved uncomfortable and hard to manage on long trips. Because it was so small, it had worn a slot in the sole of his shoe.

They would usually stay about four days, and Dad was always glad to see them leave because he called him "lazy," and remarked about how the only time he could move was when Mom announced there was something to eat.

I am sure my uncle was not lazy on his own job, but he had never lived on a farm so was not familiar with the work, and he was not the type of person who was about to learn. He would rather lay around because he was on vacation. This earned him the title of "our lazy uncle."

The Great Neighborhood Break-In

Another reason we did not like to see our lazy uncle come out for vacation was because they had a boy older and bigger than my brother and me. He was a bully and usually wrecked whatever we had to play with, so we got smart and hid most of our most treasured possessions when we knew he was coming.

One time he talked his parents into getting my parents to allow him to take the twenty-two out shooting. I remember Mom saying, "Now you boys be sure to stay behind him because he is probably real careless."

We went down the hollow and he was shooting at everything. We were thankful he was not a good shot because he would even shoot at robins, which we did not approve of at all.

On our route home, we took a short cut that took us through the neighbor's abandoned farm. He shot at some pigeons on the barn. We tried to hurry him out of there because Dad had always given us orders to stay away from there so we wouldn't get blamed if anything was ever vandalized.

As we walked past the granary, we noted there was a padlock on the granary door. At about this same time, our cousin threw up the twenty-two and fired a shot at this padlock. It was probably the first thing he had hit all day, and he drilled it dead center. In doing so, the lock popped open.

My brother and me became shocked and started out of there as fast as possible. On the way home, he made us promise never to tell or he would beat us up.

We didn't sleep too good that night, even though our company did leave.

When we all gathered for noon lunch the next day, Mom said, "There's been some excitement around the neighborhood. Someone shot the lock off Joe's granary and stole about 500 bushel of oats. The phone has been busy all morning. I guess they had the sheriff over this morning to look things over."

That took care of my brother's and my appetite. We were suddenly ready to go outside.

That afternoon Dad walked down to Joe's abandoned place. My brother and I stayed out of sight all afternoon, but we just couldn't concentrate on doing anything. We wondered if the empty shell was lying on the ground where our cousin had shot. Maybe they could trace that to us because it was our gun and shells he was using. Maybe the bullet was there and they could trace it to our gun.

We were perhaps eleven and thirteen years old, and we were really scared we might have to go to jail.

We just couldn't understand the oats being stolen unless someone came during the night and found the lock broken and helped themselves. "Boy, why did we ever go with that dumb cousin anyway?"

We thought that if we ever got out of this and he came out again, he could do everything by himself.

We had to make our appearance to get the cows and help milk. Milking was always a time when many situations were discussed, so Mom asked Dad what he heard that afternoon down to the scene of the crime.

"Well," Dad said, "the lock had been shot off all right and Joe said there were truck tracks backed up to the granary, but I couldn't see any truck tracks and I also couldn't see where he was missing any grain. I helped haul grain in there when he threshed and it don't look like any 500 bushel missing from what we hauled in."

Dad got up to walk out and dump his milk, and he stopped right in between my brother and me. He said, "Did you boys cut across through Joe's when you came back from down in the hollow yesterday?"

One thing we had been taught very well was never to lie. We just squirmed a little further under the cow we were milking and after a little hesitation and a stern, "Well, did you now?" from Dad, one of us did come out with a weak, "Ya."

"Who shot the lock?" was the next question Dad asked.

"We didn't do it. It was that darn Bud. He shot it before we knew what he was aiming at," was our reply.

We were strongly reprimanded for cutting through the barnyard, but we were not going to be punished because we did tell the truth. They knew our cousin well enough to know he would do something like this even if we tried to stop him.

We all decided that it was best to keep quiet and let things take care of themselves. The weekly paper announced a break-in and theft of grain from Joe's abandoned farm, but it said it was covered by insurance.

Mom and Dad talked about how Joe was just crooked enough to say he'd lost some grain so he could collect something from the insurance company.

My brother and I were greatly relieved when the great neighborhood break-in eventually cooled down, and I am sure our folks were, too.

Cousins with author (with bat) and brother Bud (far left)

The Cousins

We children enjoyed having our city relatives come for a visit in the summer because they were new to this kind of life and it was every day to us. It made us feel extra special when we could pet and handle animals that they were scared to go near. We especially enjoyed our one cousin. She was a couple of years younger than my brother and me, and she would always stay for a couple of weeks. Why she did it I will never know because we were always playing tricks on her and giving her a real rough time.

We milked by hand and we often tricked her into milk squirting range. She would get so gun-shy she would hardly come into the barn while we were milking.

We had kittens around the barn and she was always playing with them, so we asked her if she had ever seen a kitten drink milk, as we squirted it directly from the cow to it. After a lot of promises, we would finally get her to pick up a kitten and bring it close enough so we could squirt milk to it. Just about the time we got the kitten eating good, the temptation would get too great and we would let a good powerful stream go right into her face again.

We were just downright mean to her.

I think she liked the farm because she could go barefooted. When the opportunity afforded itself, my brother and I would each get her by an arm. We would then pull her to a real fresh cow pie. We would get her and the cow pie between us and then start pulling her back and forth. She would jump and scream to try to keep from stepping in the cow pie. This would keep up until she would finally lose her balance and step in the middle of the squishy mess.

Many hot days in the summer we would fill empty galvanized tubs with water. We would set them on opposite corners of the house. By evening, the water was warm, and using tin cans as containers, we would have water fights. By having the tubs on opposite sides of the house, we always had easy access to ammunition. My brother and I would each guard a tub, and when our sisters or cousin tried to get water, we would soak them. By directing the water specifically at their face, we could usually hold them off for quite some time. It was our only means of taking a bath, such as it was, after a hot day on the farm.

Dad's Home Brew

Our farm was located about sixty miles west of Madison, Wisconsin. Madison was the capitol of Wisconsin. We made a visiting trip there once. We had a 1929 Chevrolet that was almost new and we left very early in the morning. Dad really got confused among the street cars and traffic lights. He finally became lost and it took many, many stops of inquiry to get us to our destination. We had gone to visit relatives and it was a memorable day to us children because we had never seen street cars, stop signs, or black people. We remembered it as a great experience, but we were sure glad to be back home where we could once again enjoy the unrestricted freedom we were so accustomed to.

I am sure it was a very upsetting experience for my dad because he never went back until he was older and had driven in more traffic.

Our Madison relatives would come to visit us each summer. In preparation for their visit, Dad would make a batch of "home-brew" beer and bottle it. My one uncle would always notify us far in advance when he was coming because he said Dad made the best "home-brew" he had ever tasted.

The brew was mixed and left set in a big earthen crock. It was then siphoned off into dark-colored beer bottles and capped with a capping machine. It was then put in our basement. The basement was merely a hole dug under part of the big old farm home. The walls were laid up rock and the floor was bare earth.

There were no windows. The beer was placed on shelves in this basement and said to be left alone as it "worked."

Some of it must have worked too hard because there were occasions when we were alarmed by a terrific explosion in the basement. Upon investigating, we would find pieces of bottle glass scattered all around the basement. Fortunately, this never happened when someone was down there getting some canned goods.

When the beer had worked enough that it was ready to drink, we would carry a few bottles down and put them in the spring water in the spring house. In the evening, Dad would have a bottle and Mom would give all of us children a taste from her bottle.

One very hot afternoon, Mom sent one of us children down to the spring to get a bottle of beer as a treat to divide among us. There were four of us, plus her, at that time to divide the bottle. This didn't amount to much for each, and my oldest sister really put up a fuss because she didn't get enough. This kept up until my Mother got disgusted and said, "Well, go get a bottle and drink it all yourself then!"

She went down and got a bottle and she did drink most of it herself. We then decided to go down to the creek below the barn and go wading. The water in the creek was only ankle deep but the mud was equally as deep, so it seemed quite challenging to us.

My sister must have been about eleven years old at the time. We were only at the creek a few minutes when she began getting kind of goofy and laughing a lot. We didn't pay too much attention until she began falling around in the water and mud, and said she was real dizzy. My brother was nine and I was seven. We had never seen anyone drunk so didn't know just what was wrong, but when she began falling and getting all muddy and unable to stand up, we knew something was wrong with her. We sent the smaller sister to the house to get Mom, and we proceeded to help get her out of the mud and water. We were helping her stumble and fall in the direction of the house when Mom arrived. Seeing what a mess her oldest daughter was made Mom quite disgusted. I can remember her saying, "It just serves you right. Maybe next time you won't try to make such a pig out of yourself when we have some beer."

Mom put her on a blanket in the shade in the back yard and she slept until supper time. We were greatly relieved to know she did not have some dreaded disease, and was only intoxicated from too much beer.

FOURTH OF JULY [7]

My father with his team and wagon

Work First

The Fourth of July was always one of our most important days of the year. We children looked for this day with as much or more enthusiasm than we did Christmas. It usually meant we were done with the dreaded task of haying. Haying was a slow, dull drag that seemed to take so much out of many of the nice days of summer.

Small sections of hay would be mowed, then allowed to dry. It then had to be raked into rows called "windrows." A hay loader was then hooked on behind the hayrack. The entire long length of machinery was pulled by horses because we did not have a tractor at that time. The horses and wagon were driven straddling the windrows and as they went under the hayrack, the hay loader picked up the hay with a continuous web riding on long wooden slats. This hay loader was quite high and slanted up over the hayrack. The hay was carried up this and dropped into the hayrack where it had to be forked around by hand into a shapely load. When you had a load, a rope on the loader was jerked and the loader released and was left in place. The load was then taken to the barn. A large door was opened on one end of the barn and you drove the load under this opening.

An iron track ran the full length of the roof of the barn on the inside. A sort of trolley ran along this track and a huge fork locked into this trolley. This trolley and fork was moved by ropes attached to it. Dad would pull the trolley and fork to his end of the barn where the track extended out of the barn over the load

131

of hay. When the trolley hit the end of the track, it released the fork, and through more ropes and pulleys, the fork was pulled down to the load. Dad would stick the two-tined fork into the load of hay. He would then lift two levers on the fork that made steel projectors protrude out into the hay. These projectors were what held the hay onto the fork. When he had the ropes and pulleys clear and the fork set, he would yell, "Go ahead."

A heavy rope ran from the fork through pulleys up and along the track of the barn, then down to a pulley and post on the ground on the other side of the barn. Here a horse was hooked to the rope and when Dad said, "Go ahead," we had to walk the horse along to pull the fork full of hay up and into the barn. When the fork full of hay hit the track and trolley, it locked into the trolley and its momentum carried it along the track across the barn.

Another of us kids had to stand inside the barn, and when the fork full of hay reached the right spot in the barn, we had to yell, "Drop." At that time Dad would jerk a light rope attached to the fork, and the projectors he had set on the fork would fold in, allowing the hay to release from the fork.

It would usually take from six to nine forks of hay to unload a hayrack, sometimes more or less depending on the texture of the hay and how well it held together.

After the load was put into the barn, Dad would have to go in and spread it around evenly. This was a heavy, hot job and Dad always came out dripping wet with perspiration.

Mother guided the single horse that pulled up the fork of hay until we children became old enough. She also always helped Dad spread the hay inside the barn.

It was a very workable operation, but boring to children that would rather have been playing.

When we were too small to handle the horse or spread the hay, we had to carry drinking water or help Dad pull the rope back. When we got older, we took over Mother's jobs, and although she always helped somewhere, she did have a little more time to devote to meals, canning, and gardening.

Each time a load of hay was put into the barn, a small pail of salt was spread on the hay. If the hay was a little damp, more salt was added. This was supposedly to help keep the heat down in the hay. If the hay was not quite dry enough when it was put into the barn, it would create heat. I can remember getting up in the morning and seeing the vapor coming out of the big opening in the side of the barn. It was then that Dad would become quite concerned about the hay overheating. He would run his arm down into the hay to check it over and sometimes we would have to dig out the center of the hay because it was too hot. We would spread this to the outer edges of the barn and put more salt in the center.

Almost every year, someone's barn would burn because of the hay becoming overheated.

Spending our Allowance

If Dad thought our hay was overheating while it cured in the barn, he would delay putting any more in the barn until it cooled down. This was always a welcome break to us kids.

As the Fourth of July approached and the haying was getting wound up, we kids tried to display our best behavior. We knew the Fourth meant a trip to Grandma and Grandpa's.

It was not easy to treat our sisters in a respectful manner, but we were careful because every time we slipped a little, we were threatened with, "If you kids don't behave, we aren't going anywhere on the Fourth."

This threat was held over our heads for weeks every year before Christmas and the Fourth of July.

Grandpa and Grandma lived about thirty miles away on the edge of a small town called Lone Rock. This was located right beside the Wisconsin River. I doubt if the town had a population of five hundred people, but they put on the greatest Fourth of July celebration of any place around the area. They had a parade with clowns, and the streets were lined with chance stands of all kinds.

My uncle always had a stand of chance. He wore a carpenter's apron to keep his money in and would try to get my brother and me to buy three balls for a dime. If you knocked all the wooden milk bottles off the stand, you got a pick of prizes. The prizes were mostly big teddy bears and dolls, and we weren't interested in either. Sometimes he would have a "throw the ring stand." He would have a bunch of wooden pegs on a large flat board. You would get five rings for a nickel, and the object was to throw the rings around the pegs.

Many times, when we walked by his stand, he would give us a bunch of rings to try to win something free. We were never successful at ringing a peg, but before we left, he would probably give each of us a balloon or a tin whistle.

We never really knew how much we would get to spend at the Fourth of July celebration. We were kept in suspense until we arrived and were turned loose.

One Fourth of July remains outstanding in my memory. My brother and I were a little older, probably ten and twelve, and had put some extra effort into haying and cutting weeds just before the Fourth. We even made an extra effort to get along with our sisters, which had to have been a noted accomplishment.

We discussed and wondered what we would get for spending money. We were sure it would be a quarter each, but we never really knew until the last second before we went down the street.

When we arrived in downtown Lone Rock and got out of the car, we just sort of hung close. We were real anxious to get going down the street, but we never dared ask for any money, so we just had to wait until it was offered to us.

Finally Dad said, "Well, I suppose you boys want some money?"

We said, "Ya, suppose so."

"How much do you want?" he would say.

We always had a good idea of what we would like, but we never had the courage to come out with a figure.

We had really talked over that we would like a quarter apiece today, but neither of us could bring ourselves to ask for it.

Dad would begin to dig around in the coin compartment of his two-compartment folding-bag purse.

"Is a nickel apiece enough?" he would say.

I am sure the look of disillusionment that engulfed our face was enough of an answer, but we wouldn't utter a sound.

Our facial expressions changed considerably as we noticed Dad snap the metal snap that closed the coin section of his bag purse and unsnap the section that held the bills. We had seen Dad do this enough times that we knew one compartment from the other.

Dad pulled out a folded up bill and unfolding it he said, "Here, you can divide this between you."

I am sure our eyes were as big as saucers because we were elated to think we had fifty cents each for spending money. We had never had that much money apiece in our entire lifetime.

Both Mom and Dad firmly emphasized the fact that we should count our change carefully after each purchase because the guys that run the take a chance stands were not to be trusted, and they would short change us if we didn't watch it closely. They also made it clear that just because we had fifty cents apiece didn't mean we had to spend it all on this day.

We ran down the street a distance out of sight of the rest of the family. There we stopped. Because my brother was the oldest, they had given him the dollar bill. He reached in his pocket and took it out and gave it to me to look at and feel. It felt so good to just stretch and crinkle it. We both agreed it would be nice to keep it just like it was forever, but just ahead were too many temptations.

Walking with one hand in his pocket holding the bill, my brother took the lead down into the heart of the excitement of the Fourth of July. We decided there was no way we were going to spend all this money in one day. We agreed that we would spend a quarter each and save a quarter each for future use.

We began to roam the streets. There were all kinds of stands and the operators would follow us with, "Everybody wins at this stand; there are no losers!" The temptations were almost overpowering at times, but we held tight to our money and moved on.

Finally we got down toward the business district of town and we spotted some kids eating huge ice cream cones. This was just too much, so we decided to get an ice cream cone. We checked out both places that sold cones and watched to see which was giving the largest cones. When we decided on one, we then had to choose what flavor we wanted.

Raspberry ripple had recently been introduced into the ice cream market, and I knew this would be my choice. The cones were a nickel each and I shall never forget the problem we had when we received our change.

We had never made a purchase with this much money and we well remembered what Mother had said about making sure we always received our proper change.

We knew we should have ninety cents coming back when we bought two nickel cones. The clerk counted the change as they normally do by first saying, "Ten," meaning the cones cost ten cents. Then, by placing the remainder in my brother's hand, one at a time she counted out up to a dollar.

We had never had this happen before and it really confused us because we couldn't understand that when we had ninety cents coming back, why didn't she just count us out ninety cents.

It was evident she could see the confusion on our faces, so she started over patiently, beginning, "The cones cost ten cents, didn't they?"

We agreed with a nod of our heads. "Okay," she said, "we start out with that ten and count to a dollar."

This time my brother gave her a confused, but satisfactory nod, and we left.

We moved just out of sight of the clerk where we bought the ice cream and we stopped to count the change. We were greatly relieved to find we had ninety cents.

We were still a little disappointed because with the coins she had given us, it was not possible to divide the change equally.

The cones were so good and big that when we finished them, we decided that maybe if we each got another cone, we might get enough change to equally divide what we had left.

By the time we met the folks to watch the parade, we were on our third ice cream cone. We had not spent any money on anything else.

Mom asked what we had bought and we told her, "Three ice cream cones."

"Well," she said, "you may as well get your fill of ice cream while you have the chance; that is better than throwing it away in those gyp joints."

It didn't seem it could ever happen, but the fourth big double-dip cone satisfied our want for ice cream.

Before we left that day, we went to our uncle's stand and bought a nickel's worth of firecrackers each. He gave both of us a very generous amount.

We went home with twenty-five cents apiece in our pockets, tired, and full of ice cream.

Firecracker Fun

In the evening, when the chores were done, Dad always liked to play with firecrackers, so he would usually get a good supply from our uncle. This meant we had firecracker fun a long time after the Fourth of July.

There on the farm, far from everything and everyone, we devised everything possible to do with firecrackers. We must have been quite careful because we never had an injurious accident nor caught anything on fire with them. We came close enough to sting our fingers a couple of times, but that only made us more cautious. We did put quite a strain on the match supply, but Mother and Dad never made any big issue over it.

We would take our firecrackers when we went cutting weeds. When we got to a six-foot bull thistle, we took our jackknives and dug a hole under the roots of the thistle. We then stuck a firecracker under the roots of the thistle and touched it off. I am sure it took us half an hour and a dozen firecrackers before the final one went off and excitingly tipped the big plant over.

We would also take our firecrackers down to the creek and try to dynamite fish. All that was in the creek was a bunch of chubs, and during the hot summer weather, you could toss a small piece of wood on the water and a dozen would come up grabbing at it, thinking it was a grasshopper.

We would catch a few grasshoppers and toss them on the water and get the chubs feeding good. Then one of us would hold a firecracker and the other would light it. By careful timing and watching the fuse burn, we could toss that firecracker so it would explode just about the time it hit the water. This was also the time the chubs thought this to be another grasshopper. If everything was timed just right, we might blow up and kill three or four chubs. This only worked about once in a pool before the fish became educated and failed to respond anymore.

We would chase gophers in their holes in the ground and light firecrackers and drop them into the hole. We would then put a rock or board over the hole and stand on it to drive the explosion down. We had visions of driving the gopher out of the hole. We never got any to come out, but I am sure we gave plenty of them headaches.

Once we got the idea to build a firecracker gun. We got an elbow of pipe from Dad's scrap pile of iron. The elbow was shaped like the letter *L*, so it made a perfect looking pistol. We went to the woodshed where we selected a piece of hard oak that we used to carve a plug for the butt end of our pistol. We drove this in the back end real tight. We then used part of the same stick to cut off a piece and carve it to fit snugly in the barrel end of our gun. Our plans were to have one hold the gun and plug. The other was to light the firecracker and drop it down inside the pipe. As soon as this was done, the other was to jam the plug into the end and aim the gun.

We made a few dry runs to get our timing set. We were ready; light the firecracker, drop it in the pipe, slam projectile in place, and aim the gun. Everything had to be timed real close to work smooth.

It did, and we aimed at the barn. We were probably a good seventy-five feet from the barn when the gun went off. We didn't even see the projectile go, but we did hear it hit the barn and come bouncing back on the ground. We found it again, and upon checking the siding of the barn, we found a very distinct, deep mark where we had hit.

We were greatly excited now. We had made a gun that would really shoot. We decided we better get away from any buildings with windows, so we went out by the granary because it did not have windows.

The granary was full of mice, so we decided we would go shoot mice. We went inside the granary where there were always a lot of mice running around. We didn't have to wait long to see a mouse, but by the time we got our gun loaded and ready to fire, the mouse was gone and we had to discharge the gun into the side of the granary. We soon found this proved to be pretty dangerous inside the building because when that gun went off, the white oak plug rattled all over the granary before it settled in a bin of oats. We felt lucky it didn't hit one of us. We moved our operation outside again.

The granary was old and had cracks all around the outside. When we were inside, trying to shoot mice, we had pushed some of the oats out a couple of cracks, and this attracted a bunch of chickens. Though we were quite a distance from the chickens, we decided we would shoot into the flock just to scare them. We loaded up the gun, aimed, and fired.

If you have ever had any experience with chickens, you know how excitingly dumb they can be. If they are bunched up and one becomes excited, the entire flock goes berserk. That is what happened when we fired our firecracker gun into this flock of chickens. The entire flock just exploded. That is, all except one. One was still on the ground going around in a circle, hollering its head off and flapping its wings. We almost panicked and took off running, but we did have enough realization to know we had to get rid of our poor victim. We ran over, and catching up with the threshing hen, we grabbed her and tossed her as far as we possibly could under the granary.

It was not unusual for a hen to occasionally crawl under the granary and die, so we just thought that when this one was found, no one would be the wiser, so we took our gun and headed for the woods.

A few days later, we were eating supper when Dad said, "I wonder what happened to one of our nice laying hens. She is walking around with her head swollen so big she can't hardly see. I wonder if a cow didn't step on her." We both bowed our heads a little closer into our dinner plates and were afraid to even look in Dad's direction.

We were just sure we had killed that chicken, so figuring we had been spared this tragedy, and to avert any further disasters, we retired our firecracker gun back into the scrap pile. This was probably one of the few intelligent decisions we ever made.

We treasured our firecrackers and didn't just run around haphazardly shooting them off. We usually tried to find a purpose before we used one, but once in awhile we did use a firecracker where we should have used our head first.

We had an old outside two-hole toilet. The structure was well weathered and worn, so it was full of cracks. My brother and I were now approaching the age where we were beginning to notice the difference between girls and boys and it seemed to create an interest, especially when our cousin from the big city came out to stay. We noticed she was a lot of fun and liked to tease us as much as we liked to get teased.

We tried, a couple of times, to sneak up to the old toilet and peep through the cracks when she was inside with one of our sisters. It seemed like we were always discovered and the girls would run screaming to the house. We got pretty well reprimanded for this, which probably helped promote other action.

One of us decided the next time we saw them go to the toilet, we would sneak up behind the toilet and slip a firecracker through the crack behind and below the seats of the toilet. Now if the toilet had been recently moved, things would have leaned a little more in our favor because then there would have been a bigger distance between the hole you sat on and the pile of accumulation below. As it was, the toilet had not been moved to a new excavation for some time, and the accumulation below the holes was built up quite high.

We thought nothing about consequences as we saw our cousin and one of our sisters leisurely tooling up and into the toilet.

We always had a couple of firecrackers and matches ready, so we made our move. We quietly slipped up behind the toilet and when we thought they were all sat down, we lit up a firecracker and gave it a good thrust through a knothole. It didn't make much noise, but it sure got results—results we never anticipated. Our range and velocity were exact enough to put our firecracker right in on top of the pile of accumulation of human waste that was high enough so that when our firecracker exploded, it threw you know what all over the girls and the inside of the toilet.

The girls came out screaming and hollering all the way to the house, and we were really scared that this once we might have gone too far. Thank goodness Dad was off in the fields working because if he had been around, we may have not sat down for a week. As it was, Mom called us to get down to the house immediately. She made us empty our pockets of firecrackers and matches. She then made us get the big copper boiler, put it on the stove, and carry enough water to fill it. This was so the girls could take the needed baths.

When we were through doing this and carrying enough wood to heat the water she said, "Now you each get a pail of water and scrub rag and I want the inside of that toilet scrubbed from one end to the other, and when you are through, I will be out to inspect it."

When we saw and smelled the inside of the toilet, we decided we would rather have had the whipping because one of the holes had evidently not been covered and the entire toilet was splattered.

Our cousin laughed about it later, but she said she hoped to never have to experience a mess like that again in her lifetime.

JIMMY ^{8}

One of the many coon hounds Dad had

Our New Dog

It was early summer of 1932, when I was six years old, that something happened on the farm that was to influence my life for many future years.

My mother made an announcement that day that Dad had gone to an auction with the neighbors in hopes of buying a 1929 Model-A pickup truck. A lot of excitement was generated with the hopes that we would have a truck on the farm.

With five of us kids watching and listening for Dad to return, the afternoon became a drag.

It was getting late and near chore time when somebody yelled, "There's a car coming!"

My brother and I rushed down the path and out past the springhouse so we could see farther up the lane road. Sure enough, far down the lane we could see a strange car approaching. As the vehicle drew near, we verified it to be a pickup. A little closer and someone else excitedly yelled, "There's somebody with Dad."

As the new (to us) truck rattled across the gravel of the stream bed below the house, someone else exclaimed, "No, that's not a person with Dad; it's a dog!"

Our cow dog, Shep, was presently almost immobile with old age. He spent most of his time sleeping in a dugout excavation in the woodshed. He could not hear and made no attempt to get the cows anymore. So this unlikable chore was put on my brother and me, and we were unhappy because the cows were gradually becoming accustomed to the absence of a dog. They found they could linger all over the big woods until we found and chased them out one at a time. This extra effort was really cutting into our leisure time.

Little did we know, Dad had been secretly keeping his eye open for a cow dog.

It seemed the people who had the auction had heard Dad was looking for a dog. They were leaving the farm and wanted the dog to remain on a farm and receive plenty of tender loving care from a family with children. They slipped the dog into the cab of the pickup just before Dad left the auction.

The dog and pickup created a bountiful day of excitement, and chores were running late by the time everyone had inspected everything.

The new dog touched my heart immediately, but I could not help but think of the tearful loss this dog must have meant to the children of the other family.

The dog was a mixed breed of collie and shepherd, and had been named Jimmy.

Jimmy was about a year old, and although he was now frightened and disoriented, we were to find Jimmy still bubbling with puppy love.

Since the dog was in strange surroundings, and only about five miles from its home, Dad felt it best we keep him tied for a few days.

Jimmy meekly accepted the collar and confinement, but his facial expression changed from one of periods of happiness to one of all sorrow.

Jimmy had been taken from a family of happiness to one of strange faces and surroundings, and now to be confined on a leash created an entire new world uncomfortable to him.

I felt so sorry for Jimmy; I spent every possible minute I could close to him to ease his discomfort. I sneaked scraps from the table and, hiding them in my pants pockets, I would rush through my meal so I could hurriedly be back outside near my new dog.

At first Jimmy only looked at the scraps I brought him and did not eat them. I was sure he was going to starve to death. It wasn't until the third day of Jimmy's confinement that he gave me a weak wag with his tail as I approached him. He carefully took the scraps from my hand and cautiously ate them. When Jimmy had finished his pilfered scraps, he warily licked my hand. This sent a chill up my spine that must have shown on my face. It brought with it a slight change of facial expression in Jimmy, who seemed to now glow with affection.

On the fourth day, Jimmy finally confided in me enough to crawl up and put his muzzle on my leg. I rubbed his ears and leaning down close, I quietly tried to tell Jimmy that he would soon be able to be loose and run and play with me. Jimmy raised his head slightly and while looking me straight in the eyes, he moved his face close to mine and gave me a tender puppy kiss. I threw both arms around Jimmy's neck and from then on, we were inseparable friends.

Jimmy kept a continuous eye on the kitchen door and when I come out, he wiggled and shook all over.

I kept up a constant pressure on Dad to give me permission to allow Jimmy his freedom. After about a week, and with a promise that I would not take my eyes off Jimmy, Dad finally said, "Well, okay, but you better tie him at night for a while."

It didn't take me long to get the message to Jimmy. He seemed to understand what was going to happen and was so excited, I could hardly unsnap the chain that held him. He joyfully ran in circles around me, and on the completion of each circle, he jumped on me to show his appreciation.

Jimmy never left my side when I was outside. When I went in to eat a meal, I was constantly jumping up and checking to make sure Jimmy was still outside by the front door. He waited patiently for me to finish my meal and hopefully bring a few scraps for him.

The last thing I did before I went to bed was the painful task of tying Jimmy. He knew when I said, "Come on, Jimmy, time to go to bed," that he had to be tied. With his head and tail hanging low, he would unhappily follow me to the chain out by his house.

The first night I sat by my upstairs window watching Jimmy and waiting for him to go to bed in his house. For a long time he sat upright watching our house. He finally laid flat on his stomach facing and watching the house. He then laid his head on his two outstretched front paws, still facing the house.

I had sat on the floor and rested my head on the windowsill as I watched Jimmy. How I longed to be out there to comfort him, or better still, have had him in my bedroom with me.

I awoke with a start as I found I had gone to sleep on the windowsill. It was too dark to see Jimmy now, and anyway, the infringing sleepiness had soothed my sorrow enough to make me jump into bed and want to go to sleep.

I was awake at daybreak and back to the window. At first I felt a shock of fright because I could not see Jimmy. As my eyes focused sharper, I could see the chain leading into his doghouse and faintly make out the color of his coat. I was greatly relieved and popped back into bed to finish my sleep.

Jimmy's night confinement only lasted a week because Jimmy was now a constant companion of my brother and me, which was joyfully opening up a whole new world of boyhood dog adventures.

Adventures Down the Hollow

The arrival of Jimmy opened up a whole new world for me. It was the world of adventure into what we called the "hollow."

The "hollow" was a deep valley starting with the little stream from the spring on our farm, and as it moved along, it was joined by other small streams. As the main stream enlarged, so did the valley that engulfed this build-up of water. Huge boulders framed the wooded hillsides along the stream, and chubs and minnows abounded in the stream. It was a boyhood utopia, but I was never allowed down into it alone. I could go only as far as our land extended.

Dad and Mother had taken us farther down a few times when they went fishing chubs, but we never disobeyed the orders of going there alone. This was partly because of the neighbor's bull. He pastured his cattle in the area and, like everyone else of that era, there were times he had a bull running loose.

As spring arrived, my brother and I would begin begging for permission to extend our boundaries of exploration farther down the hollow.

It was after Jimmy's heroic act of saving Dad from the bull that Mother finally gave in one day with, "Well, okay, if you take Jimmy, watch out for Joe's bull, and make sure you don't go any further than Old Joe's land."

Old Joe owned the farm next to us and although he wasn't that old, one of us had given him this name and it stayed with him.

We were thrilled because all the good area was on Old Joe's farm, and we wouldn't have wanted to go farther.

It was on a hot day in mid-summer when my brother and I got our go-ahead and, of course, fishing was the utmost thing on our mind. Mother said, "Well, okay, but you're going to have to get your poles and rig them up yourself."

We were excited and not worried because we had seen her and Dad do this before, so we knew what had to be done. We took the dull butcher knife and went below the house to the stand of enormous willow trees. The long, straight, slender shoots that erupted all around the base of the big willows provided us with an unlimited choice of poles. When we made our selection, one would bend the shoot down and the other would hit it a sharp blow at the base with the dull knife. It would pop off and all we had to do was to brush off a few sparse leaves and small twigs. We usually selected something about six foot long.

A groove was cut around the tip of this pole, and a piece of white string that was saved from the opening of a sugar or flour sack was tied to the pole in this groove.

Dad had an old kettle full of odds and ends in his shop. We were allowed to dig through this until we found a washer or a real small nut. This was tied on the line for a sinker.

He also had a tin box of hooks, but we were never allowed in those, so either he or Mother had to tie on the hook.

We were told we had to get our own worms, and also told this might be quite an accomplishment this time of year because it had been some time since we had a slow, soaking rain to bring the worms up. We were not concerned because we had recently discovered a secret worm-getting place.

The granary on our farm was very old. When it was built they had piled stacks of flat, limestone rocks which were used as supports to hold the building up off the ground. These stacks of rocks were spaced about six feet apart, and though they had settled, they still held the granary up about two feet off the ground. During the heat of summer, this granary provided a cool sanctuary for the chickens.

It is the nature of chickens to dust, and they did this under the granary. This consisted of scratching and wiggling their bodies down into the dust. In doing so, they would eventually wear deep holes under the granary. Some of these holes threatened the rock supports, so Dad would cover the dusting holes with any old board or tin debris he could find.

One day my brother and I had spotted a big, fat toad near one of these pieces of debris. As we went to catch it, it jumped under a large piece of tin. We raised the tin and besides finding the toad, we found the cool, dark, damp ground under the tin covered with earth worms.

We had also recently found a stub of a hollow tree that held a nest of flickers. By piling some rocks against the tree, we could stretch high enough to see the young birds down deep in the hole in the tree. We noticed that whenever one of the parents landed on the edge of the hole to feed the young, the young stretched their necks and brought their heads to the edge of the hole. We took a stick and lightly tapped beside the hole in the tree. Sure enough, the young, thinking it was a parent, stretched their heads, opened their mouths, and begged pitifully.

It was then we remembered the worms under the granary. We would get a handful of worms, quietly crawl up on the rock pile and when ready, we would tap the tree. The hole would fill with large, ugly, hungry mouths, and we would drop in nice big delicious worms.

I am sure that probably turned out to be the fattest, fastest growing brood of young that pair of flickers ever raised.

It was no problem for each of us to fill one of Dad's tin, flat, velvet tobacco cans with fishing worms.

After the first trip to the "hollow," Jimmy's built-in intuition seemed to always tell him when we were getting prepared to go again. He always smiled and wiggled with eager enthusiasm as we made preparations.

When we went on these safaris, Jimmy always moved out in front of us, and there he carried on a constant patrol. He chased squirrels, chipmunks, and woodchucks. I never saw Jimmy catch any of these animals, so I really don't know if he was chasing them for fun or if he thought he was protecting us. It seemed every time he chased one of these animals into seclusion, he would return to us with a smile. He would then jump on us as if to say, "There now, it won't bother you."

One day we heard Jimmy bark up ahead of us. The bark had what seemed to be an urgency of danger. Since Jimmy seldom barked and since this was noticeably different, we speeded up our pace toward him. When we could see Jimmy, we noticed he was more excited than we had ever seen him, and the hair around the ruff of his neck was standing upright. Jimmy's attention was centered in the grass along the creek bank and he was circling and barking at something on the ground. As we got closer, Jimmy would move in front of us as much as to say, "Stay back, I'll handle this!"

Edging closer, we soon discovered the source of excitement. There, coiled on the bank of the stream, was a huge, ugly, gray water snake. As Jimmy circled the snake looking for an opening, the snake followed Jimmy by pivoting its head and continually facing him.

We thought every snake to be deadly poison, so we were greatly concerned over the safety of our dog. We tried to call Jimmy off his attack, but he would not pay any attention to us. Since we could not get Jimmy away, we decided to help. We quickly ran to the creek bank and grabbed some good-sized throwing rocks. Because of the excitement, the first few missed, but finally one did find its mark. It knocked the snake off balance and quickly gave Jimmy the opportunity he had been waiting for. He lunged in, and curling his lips back out of danger, he grabbed the snake in his teeth and gave it a quick snap and fling. Before the snake could regain its defensive position, Jimmy had it again and again. The snap and fling continued until the snake began to come apart.

Jimmy did not regain his composure until he had shaken that snake into many little pieces. Jimmy then plunged into the stream and enjoyed the clean, cool effect of the water.

After taking several drinks, Jimmy came out of the water, shook himself off, and with a look of pride and accomplishment, he came bounding up to us as much as to say, "There, I took care of that, didn't I?"

Getting the Cows

We would take Jimmy with us to get the cows, and after a couple of trips of seeing us throw sticks and hearing us yell at those stupid animals, Jimmy quickly soon caught on to our intentions. It wasn't long before Jimmy found out the cows were afraid of him and would run if he chased them. This was really fun, and each night our journey after the cows grew shorter, while Jimmy's grew longer.

Before the summer was over, all we had to say was, "Go get 'em," and Jimmy was off on another of his fun-loving activities of chasing cows.

At a certain time of the year, Dad had the bull running with the cows. The bull had a disagreeable temperament that had to be watched carefully. Jimmy's first experience with the bull and its temperament happened one of the first days of the bull's release.

Jimmy always herded the cattle and brought them into the barnyard by following along behind them. If one slowed down a little more than Jimmy thought was too pokey by his standards, he would slip up behind it and nip it on the heel. Perhaps the bull had just a touch more intelligence or alertness than the cows, or maybe Jimmy had a bad day. At any rate, on this day as Jimmy brought the herd in, the bull was lagging behind a little. Just as Jimmy slipped up to nip the bull on the heel, the bull must have seen him coming and let drive with a quick-flying hoof. The hard hoof of the bull caught Jimmy right under the chin and sent him flying into a dusty blur on the path.

My heart skipped a couple of beats when I heard the sickening thud and saw Jimmy roll. When the dust cleared, Jimmy was getting to his feet. He shook himself off and then realizing what had happened, his shepherd temper erupted. He now took after the bull in a much more careful, determined manner. The bull was quite confident now and almost reluctant to move. Every time Jimmy made an advance, the bull would swing around facing Jimmy. This seemed to satisfy Jimmy because he just made a quick dart in and nipped the bull on the nose. This only happened once, and the bull turned around. Jimmy watched close, and whichever way the bull was looking back, Jimmy would quickly dart in from the opposite, blind side, and nip the bull on the heel. It only happened a couple of times before the bull took off to gain the protection of the herd in front of him.

Jimmy never forgot the rap he got from the bull. Every chance he had, he would single out the bull for a little added harassment.

Jimmy Comes to Dad's Aid

Maybe this little animosity between those two animals prevented a happening that could have had a catastrophic influence on our entire family.

When Dad was through with the bull servicing the herd, he would then separate the bull from the herd. Sometimes the bull was tied in the orchard, and sometimes he was put in the small pasture with the two horses.

On this particular day, the bull was in the pasture with the horses. Dad went out to drive the horses in and in doing so, he must have unknowingly got himself out a little too far away from the surrounding fences. At about this same time, the bull noticed Dad's vulnerable position. Dad started to run for the fence the same time the bull started for Dad.

By now Jimmy had been around our farm long enough that he was quite used to playing the role of boss. If a chicken flew over the fence into our house yard, Jimmy harassed it until it flew out or we opened the gate and helped him chase it out.

If a pig got out of the pig yard, Jimmy loved nothing better than to annoy it enough to keep it squealing until we arrived to help get it back where it belonged.

On this particular day of Dad's predicament, Jimmy must have been again watching over his flock, because as Dad related the story, he could feel the bull's hot breath on his back. The fence seemed miles away when a yellow, growling, snarling, flash came ripping past and flew into the bull with a fury. Dad

Bull on farm

Cows on farm

said, "I was never so glad to see a dog in my life because I never would have made it to the fence in time."

We used to love to hear Dad relate his narrow escape from the bull because it made us so proud of the newly acquired member of our family.

Same two as on cover of book during WW II

Playing Games With Jimmy

Jimmy loved to tease us into his game of tag. He would grab a mitten or cap, then run in circles. These circles always included coming close enough to us so we could touch him, but not close enough to catch him. He loved to have us chase him. He would remain poised flat out on the ground with the piece of clothing in his mouth. As soon as we would get close enough to make a lunge at whatever he had, he was up and away again. This was kept up until we finally changed our tone of voice and demanded he give back what he had. He seemed to understand the game was over and he would give back the garment.

If we went sledding or skiing, Jimmy would race along beside us, having as much fun as we did. If we took a tumble and lost a cap or mitten, he would grab it and race off with it. It would then take some harsh words to make him release it, and understand we weren't playing tag now, and we needed our garment to keep warm.

Many evenings in the summer we would play hide and seek with Jimmy. One of us would hold him and the other would run and hide. When the other person was hidden, we would release Jimmy and say, "Find him; go find him." Jimmy would take off as fast as his legs would carry him. We confined our play to the house yard, so there were only so many places to hide, and Jimmy soon knew them all.

We would also run races with Jimmy. One of us would hold him and the other start to run around the house. When the runner got a good start, the other would release Jimmy and the race was on. When he caught you, he would be sure to give you a good bump in such a manner as to let you know you didn't outrun him.

Jimmy Comes to My Aid

Although Dad owed Jimmy one, he was to find out that Jimmy was really boss of things around the farmstead.

This happened one time when my brother and I were up to something or into something we weren't supposed to be into. We periodically had these incidents which resulted in a "warming-up" as Dad called them. A "warming-up" consisted of a pretty good whipping with either the leather strap that hung in the closet, or if outside, with whatever was handy.

Now, through experience, we learned that the louder you yelled and the more expressive you carried on, the shorter the whipping lasted. On this day, this learning experience was taking place in the barnyard. My brother had already had his "warming-up" and I was getting mine. Dad had me across his knee and was giving it to me pretty good. I must have been carrying on with a top performance, or maybe Jimmy and me had a little closer relationship, because the next thing I knew I heard a growl, seen a flash of yellow, and I was dropped hard and fast on the ground as Dad straightened up, rubbing his behind.

It didn't take me long to get my feet going, and together the three of us—my brother, Jimmy, and me—were running off to our sanctuary in the woods. We ran until we reached our sacred hiding place and caught our breath. There Jimmy helped lick away the tears as the sobbing subsided.

We then compared bruises to see if either were significantly hurt. Not any worse than usual, so I asked my brother what happened.

Though it was never talked over or planned, it just seemed to fall in line that whoever got the first whipping waited for the other so they could go off with Jimmy and together compare the damage.

My brother said, "Well, Dad was really giving it to you and you were really yelling when Jimmy came up behind Dad. It looked like he nipped Dad in the behind. It was so fast I really couldn't tell for sure, but boy, he really let go of you in a hurry."

I had to grin as I rubbed Jimmy's ears and wiped my running nose on my sleeve.

The Run Away Plans

As soon as the initial shock of the whipping had subsided, we began making our usual plans to run away. We went to the hole in the bottom of the big, red oak tree and removed the rock that plugged the hole. There we took out a tin baking soda can and checked its contents. The matches, string, and jack knife were still in the can. A further check in the hole revealed our two corncob pipes, and extra leather and rubbers for slingshot repair. There was a damp match box in the hole. It fell apart as we tried to open it, but all that was in it were a few used nails, one safety pin, and a small piece of copper wire. We put these in the baking powder can. We then buried the match box in some loose dirt under the roots of another tree.

We talked about where we would run away to. We didn't really know anywhere to go, but the neighbor boy said he would like to take a log and float down to the Mississippi. We didn't know how far away the Mississippi was, but we had heard some of the grown men talk about going down there fishing, so it couldn't be too far. If we could get that far, we could then make a raft of logs and go for miles.

We would need some binder twine, but we knew if we were ever caught in Dad's shop getting binder twine, we would get worse than we got today. We would just have to wait until dark and then see what we could find.

We would need some more matches and some food anyway.

That's what we would do. Our plans were made. We sat silently thinking it all over.

I was between seven and eight years old and two years younger than my brother. I suppose this entire endeavor was much more emotional to me than to him because when I started to think more about it, and especially about leaving Mom, I began to get a big lump in my throat. I knew she would worry when we were gone, and this would hurt her and probably make her cry. It always hurt me to see her cry.

I remembered the last time I saw Mom cry was when we were picking corn. The corn was always picked by hand and they used horses and a wagon. The wagon had a "bang-board" on one side. This was nothing but a few boards that were nailed together and slipped on the side of the wagon to make the side higher. This enabled you to pick and throw without watching where the ear went. The ear would hit the bang board and fall into the wagon. You could concentrate on the ears on the stalks and you could pick faster this way.

Mom always picked one row right next to the wagon, while Dad picked the next two rows away. This way they picked three rows at a time across the field.

It was a cold day in late fall when they were picking, and Dad threw an ear for the wagon and the ear hit Mom in the head. It made a sickening sound and I knew it must have hurt.

All Dad said was, "Whoops" and he went right on picking. Mom went behind the wagon and cried. I went back there with her but I just didn't know what to say. I cried some with her, but more than anything, I wanted to take an ear of corn and hit Dad in the head. It was awhile before Mom started picking again and she had a big bruise on the side of her face for some time.

The lump would not go away as I continued to think about leaving Mom. I would miss her, especially when it came time to go to bed. It seemed the bed and blankets didn't feel right unless Mom put them down for me to get into and then fastened them back up around my head.

What if I became sick?

I was always getting sick with the flu. When this happened, I would get a high fever and when I got really bad, I would see weird things that were scary.

What would I do if Mom wasn't there to help me over these terrible scary times?

It was getting dusk and I was becoming kind of uneasy when my brother broke the silence with, "Wonder if they had supper yet?"

I said, "Maybe if we sneaked down to the edge of the woods, we could see in the kitchen window."

We put our cache back in the tree and replaced the rock cover. We then sneaked from tree to tree until we came to the edge of the woods where we could look down on the kitchen. We could see someone move past the window once in awhile, so we knew they weren't eating yet. Then I caught the aroma of fried pork. Nothing tasted better than Mom's fried pork. Mom would go upstairs to a big crock in the empty upstairs room and dig some fried-down pork out of a big earthen crock. This was preserved by putting it in big pans soon after we butchered and most of the fat was baked or fried out. The meat was then put in these earthen jars and the fat poured back over it. The fat then became solid and white, preserving the meat. The mice would run around on top of this and make tracks and dig small excavations, but this was all scraped off and thrown away when-ever we began using meat out of a new crock.

There was just nothing better than Mom's fried-down pork combined with raw fried potatoes.

The silence was broken by Mom's welcome voice, "Boys, come to supper." We sat silently. I am sure we both wanted to respond, but neither wanted to let the other know he had weak-ened.

A little while later, one sister came out and called a couple of more times, but sisters put no emotional stress on us.

The silence seemed eternal. Maybe they weren't going to call anymore. Maybe they were all done eating now and had put everything away. Maybe nobody cared if we ate or not.

I was really hungry. What were we going to do because it was getting dark real fast now?

We heard the welcome sound of the porch door opening. Was it Dad coming to give us some more whipping for not com-ing down for supper? Soon we could make out Mom coming around the corner of the house, "Come on now boys; Dad's all through eating and I want to get at the dishes."

One of us would usually come up with a weak something like, "Well, I suppose we better go so she can get the dishes done, but maybe we can get some more stuff together by tomorrow."

Jimmy seemed to be waiting just as anxiously as us, because the minute we stood up and started for the house, he was wig-gling and wagging all over, seemingly aware that everything was over now and he would get his evening meal after all.

The Trips to the Mailbox

Our mailbox was located on the county road about a half mile from our house. The road from our house out to this county road was nothing but two dusty wheel tracks. This route was taken to haul the milk to the cheese factory every other day. The route crossed the creek created by the spring, then up a gradual hill, and there the route split. You had a choice of going below or above the parallel fence. The route you then took depended on the rotation of the crops. If corn was planted in the one lower field, you would have to open two miserable wire gates to follow the lower route. If it was being pastured, you only had one gate, the same as the upper route.

The route twisted and turned up another hill and there was a nice wooden hinged gate that was on the line fence separating our farm from the neighbors. We had to open this gate and cross the neighbor's land where we joined his road practically in his farm yard. We then continued out to the county road where both our mailboxes were located.

During the summer, it was one of my assignments to get the mail each day. This was always an adventure for Jimmy and me. We carried on a continuous battle against the gophers. It wasn't until many, many years later that I found the proper name of these little animals to be "thirteen-lined ground squirrels."

We didn't particularly like the looks of the almost earless little critters, and besides, Dad always praised us every time we destroyed one, so we carried on a continuous battle against them.

They were quite destructive to a cornfield. Just as the corn began to poke through the ground, these little gophers would spot this new plant, and knowing there was still a good sized part of the seed remaining in the ground, they would dig under the plant and eat the remaining part of the seed. If one got a start at an area of a cornfield, it could wipe out quite an area before the corn outgrew the little rascal.

So, on our daily adventure trip to the mailbox, a continual surveillance was kept for gophers.

If we could run one in its hole that wasn't too far from the spring, I would plug the hole with rocks and dirt, then when I would return home, I would get my brother and we would carry water and try to drown the gopher out of its hole in the ground. Sometimes this required many trips back and forth to the spring. If you could get the hole full of water, the gopher would finally come gasping out and Jimmy would put an end to it.

There were times we would make many trips carrying and pouring, but the hole would not fill nor would the gopher come out. It was obvious the hole probably joined a crack in some limestone rock and the water had an easy escape route.

The mailbox trip took me through the neighbor's barnyard. They also had a dog, so to avoid any conflict between the two dogs, I would order Jimmy to remain by the wooden gate at the line fence. Jimmy would always give me that woebegone look as I walked on and he had to stay behind. He knew what was expected of him and obeyed faithfully. As soon as he spotted me returning, he would excitedly jump on the wooden gate and wag me a warm welcome. Never would he cross on the other side of the gate.

Leaving Jimmy for School

Summer drew to a close and with it the opening of school. This would bring with it a drastic change in Jimmy's daily routine.

The first day of school found all of us kids coming out of the house early in the morning and going down the springhouse path, out past the garden, and up toward the mailbox. Jimmy joyfully joined the procession with the anticipation of this going to be another great play day somewhere. We took turns scolding him and telling him to stay home, but this had never happened to Jimmy before, and he just couldn't understand. Not wanting to disobey but still wanting to go, Jimmy dropped back a way and with a forlorn look of misunderstanding, he followed slowly and sadly along.

This continued all the way up to where our two farms separated at the wooden gate. Here Jimmy had always waited for me when I went for the mail. What would he do today when I didn't return?

I let my brother and sisters go on and I waited by the gate. Jimmy, seeing me there alone and having been scolded more than usual this morning, hung his head and tail and sadly begged to approach me.

I had another lump in my throat as I assured him he could come up to me and I would not scold him. Jimmy wagged his tail and joyfully came rushing up and jumped all over me. I am sure he was happy to now see I was not angry. I knelt down beside him as he licked my hands and face. The lump seemed to get larger as I tried to explain to Jimmy that he had to go home because today I would not return.

Jimmy tilted his head and seemed to know today was different, but his dog brain could not tell him why.

I tried to be firm, but this was not possible without hurting Jimmy's feelings.

He finally understood and slumped down the dusty path toward home as I opened the gate. When I closed the gate he sat down and watched me. I took off running as fast as I could, partly because I didn't want to be late for the first day of school, and partly because the rushing air felt good to my tear-filled eyes.

It was a long day in school, and every recess time I was almost afraid to go out for fear Jimmy might be waiting there for me.

When school ended, I left my brother and sisters far behind as I ran to get home to see Jimmy.

As I approached the board gate where I had left Jimmy that morning, I was appalled to see that faithful dog leaping on the board gate, overjoyed that I had not let him down. I hugged Jimmy and wiped tears of joy as he ran circles of delight around me.

Mother said they had not seen Jimmy, so I knew he had waited all day, knowing I would return and not forget him.

Jimmy waited by the gate every day, and every day we had a few bread crusts for him.

We don't know when it happened, but eventually Jimmy figured out our schedule. He would accompany us as far as the gate in the morning and then return home. At about the time he knew we would return, Mother said he would go out the path and up the dusty road to meet us.

Jimmy continued his faithful after-school meetings, never missing a day during my entire grade school attendance.

It was always my firm belief that if every boy could grow up with a Jimmy, there would be no bad boys, for Jimmy's world, and everything in Jimmy's world, was filled with only love and good things.

Author with fish

FISHING 9

Our Fish Poles

It was always a fun trip to go visit Grandpa and Grandma. They lived about thirty miles from us on the outskirts of the little town of Lone Rock, near the Wisconsin River. The highlight was that we could usually go fishing when we went to visit them. In preparation for one of these trips, my brother and I would work tediously making fish poles for this once-a-summer occasion.

Our goal was the creation of a casting rod and reel. All we had to work with for reels were some large sewing spools Mother gave us, and for poles we used willow branches. The willow branches were cut green. They were limber, and while green and fresh, seemed to serve our purpose.

For line guides on the poles we used copper wire. To attach the spool to the pole for a reel, we would put a hole through the butt end of the pole and slip the spool on the nail and put the nail through the hole in the pole. We would then fasten a small screw into the side of the spool for a handle, and that was our rod and reel. If we used a heavy enough weight on the end of the line, we could, with careful effort, at times throw it out a short distance.

We worked and practiced diligently as we prepared for the trip to Grandpa's. By the time the day arrived and we got to go to the river, our green willow poles had dried out so much they had shrunk, so the copper wire we used for guides were now loose and after a couple of attempts to cast, the guides would turn all directions on the pole.

The hole through the butt of the willow stick had dried out and the nail was so loose it would fall out, and our spool with line would fall on the ground and become a mess.

We never really made a successful casting outfit, but every trip to Grandpa's resulted in hours of preparation and anticipation.

Grandpa must have felt a little sorry for us because on one of our trips, he gave us a reel and pole. The reel and pole were both very old and originally very inexpensive. The reel did not have a level wind and was simply something with a handle to wind line upon. The pole was of the same vintage.

To my brother and me, they were precious and we cherished the two pieces of fishing equipment with delight. We took them home and treasured both, for it was this summer we were to get to go to Grandpa's and stay for an entire week.

In anticipation for this vacation with Grandpa, we built more home-made casting rods and reels. From experience, we allowed the poles to dry before we equipped them. By the time we were ready to go on vacation, we had a good supply of home-made rods and reels, plus the one Grandpa gave us.

While vacationing with Grandpa, we spent all of our time along the river. This time was not very productive, but when I look back at our fishing experience, it is understandable.

Our bait consisted entirely of worms, of which we had a good supply because we dug and stockpiled for weeks ahead.

The Big Catch

Most of the fish we caught consisted of small bait-stealing shiners or catfish that were not big enough to keep. If we did hook into something of any size, it would break our weak line or pull loose before we even got a look at it.

One day we were fishing off a bank about six feet high and the current along the bank was quite swift. I guess it was my turn to use the pole with the reel on this day. I got a bite and when I set the hook, the line took off out into the river with the gusto of a large fish on the other end. Fortunately, the little reel did not jam and by spinning backward, it allowed the fish to take out line. After a few circles in the area, the fish settled down deep in the swift current directly below us. We were both very excited now because we realized we had hooked into a fish larger than we had probably ever seen in our life.

The largest fish we had ever seen were those on a fish peddler's truck. The fish peddler would come around to the farm about once a month and sell Dad fresh fish. The fish were iced down in the truck and consisted of carp, catfish, and sheepshead. The fish were usually from two to six pounds, but since our fishing was limited to small streams, we had never caught anything larger than chubs, or perhaps a foot long sucker.

Fortunately, the fish I had hooked did not decide to run up or down the river, for if it had done so, I would not have been able to stop it. I had very little line on the reel and the line was not very strong, so I had to handle the fish gently. It stayed right in front of us where the current was swift and deep. There it would make short runs, most of the time in circles.

We started getting concerned about where we were going to land this fish because the bank was high and there was no way we could reach the fish or lift it up over the bank.

After what seemed an eternal amount of time, I began to notice the fish becoming weaker. We wanted desperately to see what it was, so I began to increase the pressure and the fish began to move. It finally made a roll toward the surface and we caught a glimpse of a big flat side, indicating it was probably a carp. After getting a look at the fish, it made us more nervous because we both excitingly agreed it was the largest fish we had ever seen.

We now began to wonder how we would land this fish. My brother ran down the river and soon yelled that he found an indentation in the bank where we could get down to the water level and perhaps get at the fish. I began to work the fish down in his direction until I reached the low area. This was fine, but every time I worked the fish in toward us to the point where it noticed either us or shallow water, it would take off for deep water with added gusto. Each run wore the fish down a little more until it finally stayed close to the surface and just swam back and forth. Finally, one of us thought of stabbing it with a pocket knife. We thought if we could kill it, we could then reach into the river and lift it out.

My brother stretched out on his belly on the bank with the knife posed. This was fine, but every time I brought the fish in close, it would see him and away it would go again. Every run was now getting a little weaker until I finally got it close enough and he let drive. He stabbed the fish in the top of the head, but all it did was make the fish go wild. It took off out into the river

The prize blue buffalo

so fast I thought for sure something would break. Miraculously, everything held and the fish soon slowed down again.

As I worked the fish back, we were excited to see a red stream pouring out of the knife wound in its head. We had drawn blood and were now certain we were winning this battle.

The fish weakened fast now and it soon turned over on its side. I eased it up to my brother again, and this time when he struck with the knife, the fish was too weak to break loose. Using the knife as a lever in the fish, he was able to pull it up onto the bank. We both sat down shakingly exhausted as we looked at our catch. To a couple of country boys, it was the largest fish ever seen.

We put a stick through its gills and carrying it together, we took right off up the road to Grandpa's.

Grandpa had a way of making you feel real good when you done something he highly approved of, so when he seen us coming with the fish, he flicked that once in awhile twinkle in his eye as he said, "Well, well, you guys really done it up big today didn't you—you got yourself a right nice fish there."

Gramps had a way of saying, "You bet," that came out as one word, "Yabet." That was the same as when he said, "No sir." It always came out as one word, "Noser."

Gramps said, "Ya know what ya got there?"

We said we thought it was a carp.

"Noser," Gramps said, "you got yourself a right nice blue buffalo there."

Our next question was, "Are they any good to eat?"

"Yabet your boots they're good to eat," Gramps replied.

It made us feel real good to see Gramps so enthusiastic about our catch. "Well sir," Gramps said as he went into his neat little shop, "we better see what that fish weighs."

He came out with a small hand scale that showed signs of being well oiled over its many years of usage. He hooked the fish in the lip and held it up. It seemed it took him forever to focus his bifocals before he finally said, "Twelve pounds right on the button."

We could hardly believe that it was that big. "Gee, what would Dad think of something like this, after buying those two and three pound carp off the fish truck?"

Gramps said, "Well sir, we'll dress it out and put it right on ice in the ice box, and when he comes to get you day after tomorrow, he can take it home with him."

I am quite sure that when Dad and Mom drove up Gramps' driveway, they could tell from the beam on our faces that some-

The author, grandfather, and brother Bud with the blue buffalo

thing big had happened. We could hardly wait to show and tell about our twelve-pound blue buffalo. Dad was never much for expressing compliments, but you could tell from his expression that this once we had really done something he appreciated.

Gramps left the head on the fish so we could show the battle scars. Dad and Gramps exchanged glances of amusement as we related our blow by blow account with the fish.

Mom fixed it up as soon as we got home and I can remember Dad remarking how good it was, but to us kids, it wasn't any-different tasting than the awful carp he bought off the fish truck.

Gramps Gives Us Fishing Lessons

A couple of times while we vacationed with Gramps, he took us smallmouth bass fishing. Living within walking distance of the Wisconsin River, this merely meant putting a few things of necessity in his pockets, selecting a light cane pole from under the overhang of his garage, and with his ever-present walking cane, we were on our way.

Gramps' cane, or to express it more accurately, his walking stick, was chosen from a select limb of a hickory tree. The top, or gripping part of the stick, was worn smooth and slick from the many miles it had accompanied Gramps. It looked as antiquated as Gramps and was as much a part of him as was his ever-present chew of Red Man tobacco. You never really noticed either, but it would have been conspicuous had either been missing.

It was always entertaining when Gramps related a hunting or fishing story because his walking stick contributed as much to the story as did his quick little eyes or expressive voice.

Using his walking stick to draw out the detail on a damp, bare spot on the lawn, Gramps could take you on a coon hunt so realistic you could almost hear the hounds bark tree.

Gramps didn't offer us fish poles, nor did we see him prepare any bait. We knew from being firmly reprimanded a couple of times that you didn't vex Gramps with a lot of questions.

Gramps once told us, "If you just be quiet and watch and listen, you will not have to ask questions."

We watched and listened as we cut across a small marsh in the direction of the river. As we got deeper into the marsh, Gramps slowed down and appeared as though he was looking for something he had lost. All at once he stopped, raised his walking stick, and struck a sharp blow into the marsh grass. He then leaned over and picked up something.

"There, boys," he said, "that's going to be our bait."

He held up a small leopard frog. It looked dead. He then took out a well worn Prince Albert tobacco can from his pocket. The metal lid was punched full of holes. He dropped the frog in, closed the lid, and slipped the can back into his shirt pocket.

Gramps flattened two more frogs before we got to the river. I never saw Gramps miss a frog nor did he ever kill one. He always tapped them just hard enough to render them unconscious. He needed them alive to fish with, so while he was fishing with one frog, he always had a couple more in the can recovering from a hickory headache.

We soon found out why Gramps did not want us to take fish poles when he went smallmouth fishing. He was very discreet about where and how he fished. He might walk the bank of the river a good distance before he would come to a place of his liking. This was usually a place in the river where there was a stump, or perhaps a log, out in the river. Handing one of us his precious walking stick, he would carefully open the tobacco can and take out the most recovered of the frogs. He would tenderly hook it on and then he would quietly approach the chosen spot in the river. We were made to stay back and remain quiet. When Gramps was in the proper position, he would plunk that frog in a purposeful, attention-getting fashion, right next to the log in the river. The frog would usually get in about three powerful swimming strokes before the water would explode. It was exciting to watch the fast action that followed between that light cane pole, Gramps, and a two pound smallmouth in fast current.

We would usually cover a good half a mile of rough woods walking along the river before Gramps got his three bass. He would cut forked sticks, and it was our job to hook the fish through the gills and carry them. It was always a welcome relief to get back to the house and get a nice, fresh, cold drink of water.

It seemed nothing could surpass a meal of raw fried potatoes and a heaping pan of fried smallmouth bass.

Gramps used this same method of operation for catching large sunfish. He would swat grasshoppers with his trusty walking stick, but here again, he would never kill them. He would only stun them.

Gramps allowed us to get close enough to watch him fish the grasshoppers. This trip usually took us to one of the back waters off the river. Here he would find a tree that hung out over the water. Carefully approaching the area, he would lightly hook on a grasshopper, and using the same light cane pole that he used for smallmouth fishing, he would drop the grasshopper gently on the water under the overhanging tree. We would almost immediately see the dark form of a big bluegill ease up under the petrified grasshopper.

Gramps would say, "Be still and watch close now."

The grasshopper and bluegill would remain motionless for what seemed forever. Finally, the grasshopper would stretch out one leg, and this movement spelled doom to both of them.

These little lessons in Gramps' school of nature remained with me, and once mastered, provided me with endless hours of successful, entertaining fishing.

Fishing Chickens

The corn crib on our farm was set up off the ground on spaced apart piles of flat limestone rocks. It was just high enough for the chickens to get under, and because a few kernels of corn would occasionally shake down through the cracks in the floor, it was a popular place for the chickens to rest.

My brother and I would use the old corn crib as a shelter where we would sneak off and smoke corn silk. Corn silk was the material on the end of an ear of corn designed by nature to catch the pollen from the top of the plant. When the corn was harvested and put into cribs, this corn silk became dry. We would take a cob of corn that did not have any kernels on it and break off a piece of this cob. The center of the cob had a soft pith. We would dig out some of this pith, then work a hole through the side of the cob and insert a hollow reed. We then had a corn cob pipe that we would fill with corn silk and smoke.

Our smoking attempts were never too successful, but one day, while making another attempt, one of us noticed the chickens feeding on the corn we were knocking down through the cracks in the floor. With an ever-present high enthusiastic fishing fever, the idea of "Let's get our poles and go fishing," came up.

We rounded up our old willow stick fish poles with the sewing thread spool reels and wondered why we hadn't thought of this new venture long before.

Whenever we went to Grandpa's fishing, Dad would take the store-bought fish line off the cane poles and give it to us for our poles. When we returned, we had to give it back so he could put it back on the cane pole to be used when he went sucker fishing in the local streams.

At that time, all the sugar and flour sacks were machine sewn together on top with white cord. When you opened the sack, you cut off one end and by pulling properly, you could open the top of the bag and have two nice long pieces of string. Mom always saved all of this string because we used it for everything.

So, it was off to see Mom for some fish line for our poles. We each wound on the allowable amount she gave us and enthusiastically returned to the corn crib. We searched around until we found an ear of corn with long kernels. We then tied a kernel on the end of our fish line and dropped it down the crack in the floor. It was only a second when we had a bite. We made believe it was a fish and left the line run out as the noisy spool unwound. When we decided it was far enough, we would give a jerk and start pulling in yelling, "I got one, I got one!" The thrill was short-lived because the kernel of corn would easily pull off the string. We would lose our fish and were left with a wet, slimy piece of string.

After a few more futile attempts of always having a short battle and losing our fish, we decided we had to improve on our mode of operation.

We got out the ever-present jack knife and drilled a hole through the kernel of corn. We then ran the string through the hole and tied it on tight. We now had our confidence up and dropped the bait down again. This time when we set the hook, as they say in fishing, we really had a fish that put up a fight. The only problem was that our fish were quite noisy because they squawked and hollered furiously as the kernel of corn was reluctantly pulled back out after they had swallowed it.

It wasn't long before all of our fish were sore throat educated and we couldn't get a bite. We then began shelling corn and dropping it down the crack. At first the chickens wouldn't touch it, but it wasn't long before a bold one stepped forward and we had our fish feeding again. When things were going good, we dropped our tied-on kernels down with a handful of regular corn, and it wasn't long I yelled, "Got a bite!"

I let it run a ways and then set in for the battle. This chicken was different. It might have eaten my kernel of corn and then swallowed several more, which prevented mine from coming out, because when I started to crank my spool reel, the fish on the end went berserk squawking, hollering, and flopping around under the corn crib. The stress on my light outfit was not up to handling the pressure being exerted from the other end, and all at once, the reel came off from the pole. When it came off, it wedged against the copper wire eye on the pole. This gave the chicken a good solid support to pull against, and the next thing to give was the string going through the eyes on my pole and down the crack of the corn crib floor.

We now became quite concerned because we couldn't have Dad see this chicken running around the barnyard with a string hanging from its mouth. It would be quite obvious, "Those boys had been up to something again."

We could already feel our hinders burning.

We ran around behind the corn crib, and there we could see the chicken under the corn crib with the string hanging from its mouth. There was just no way we could get under there after it.

We decided that if we could get the chicken out, we could run it down and pull the string out. We threw rocks and everything, but the dumb chickens would not come out from under the corn crib.

Jimmy, our faithful farm dog, understood everything we told him; he loved nothing better than to chase dumb chickens, so we decided to call on his help. We thought if one of us stood on one side of the corn crib and the other sent Jimmy under, he could probably chase the chicken out and we could catch the string as it came out.

Under the corn crib were quite a few piles of limestone rocks that supported the crib. There was also some old half-buried boards and tin. Evidently, when Jimmy eagerly went under to do his job, the chickens run around under the crib in all directions before they came out. The one with the trailing string must have got the string entangled around something because when they decided to come out, they all came together, with Jimmy in hot pursuit. Before I could even gain my senses enough to try and grab the string, the chicken had reached the end of the slack it had and with a large noisy squawk, it did a complete flip in the air. Jimmy thought he had a slow mover and was about to rough it up when the chicken regained its feet, and with the help of its wings, it gave a few desperate flops that dislodged the corn and freed the bird of its fish line.

All of this commotion also brought Mom out of the house with, "What in the world are you boys doing down there?"

Our standard answer was, "Oh, nothing much."

That ended our chicken fishing adventure as we felt we were fortunate to have been able to get out of this predicament without being caught.

Pal and Me Go Fishing

The day finally arrived when I had to vacation alone at Gramps, because my brother reached the age where the neighbors wanted him to work for them in the summer. I really wasn't alone because Gramps had recently been given a little black cocker spaniel that he named "Pal." Pal and I became immediate friends. We were youthful companions from the minute we met, and every day was a new adventure down around the river.

I was now twelve years old, and old enough to be trusted to go fishing whenever I wished.

One day Gramps said, "Why don't you go catfishing? Come on in the shop and I'll fix you up."

By now I had bought a steel telescopic rod from the Montgomery Ward catalog and had the old reel fastened on it that Gramps had given us. I couldn't do any casting with artificial bait, but I could put on a hook and heavy sinker and throw out a short distance.

Gramps reached up on the shelf and took down a discolored glass jar. He unscrewed the lid, and holding it in front of my nose, he said, "What do ya think of that?"

Over a period of years on the farm, I had been introduced to all kinds of different offensive odors, but this jar smelled like something worse than I had ever encountered. My eyes watered as I drew back and said, "What in the world is that?"

"Catfish bait," was Gramps' reply.

He put the lid back on, and reaching into a small box, he took out two small treble hooks.

"Now," he said, "when you get to the river, you tie on one of these treble hooks, ball a wad of this catfish bait on it, and drop it into a deep hole and hang onto your pole, 'cause it will catch catfish."

I was kind of excited because Dad would always check the price of catfish from the fish peddler, and although he always tried to talk the guy into selling him some, they could never arrive at a negotiable price, and Dad had never come out on top with a catfish. This would be great if I could catch some catfish.

With the two hooks in the catfish bait jar and some sinkers in my pocket, Pal and I enthusiastically took off for the river.

The deepest water I could think of was around the cement abutments of the highway bridge, so that's where we headed.

To get down on the abutment from the highway, I had to crawl through the iron girders and work my way down. Knowing Pal could not climb down, I took him under one arm and carried him down. The abutments were large cement platforms and there was room for Pal to run around on top of them.

There was about a fifteen-foot drop from the top of the abutment to the water, but I was unconcerned about Pal falling in because he would not go near the edge.

I sat down, took out a treble hook, and wadded on a ball of catfish bait. I sat this down on the cement beside myself and proceeded to thread the line through my pole and fasten on a heavy sinker. When I turned to pick up the treble hook and catfish bait to tie it on my line, it was gone. I took a second look and there sat Pal with his head cocked to one side, licking his lips.

I felt like someone hit me a terrific blow right in the pit of my stomach as I realized what had happened. While I was busy with the pole, Pal had found that this catfish bait smelled very appetizing and had gulped it down, hook and all.

I quickly jumped up and began looking all around. My hopes were that maybe Pal just licked the bait off the hooks and they would be around on the cement somewhere. My effortless search only added to my building frustration. I would have given almost anything to have found that treble hook around there somewhere.

Pal seemed to be begging for more of that good bait, so I knew he had taken everything in one gulp.

I didn't really feel like fishing anymore, but I couldn't go back to Gramps or he would ask questions.

I sat on the edge of the abutment losing all interest in fishing. Pal seemed to sense something was bothering me as he put his curly black head on my lap. As I scratched his soft, silky ears, a lump formed in my throat.

This was my second day of vacation. I would have five more to spend. What would they be like?

I planned on having so much fun and now this had to happen. Should I tell Gramps? Could they operate and remove the hook from inside of Pal? Would Pal just get sick and die slowly? I heard my folks warn us about swallowing fish bones because they would get caught in our insides and we would have to have them cut out in the hospital.

All of these things were jumbling my mind. I would not have been quite so concerned had this been a single hook, but this was a treble hook, or the same as three hooks in one. I could not help but think there was no way this would dissolve, nor was there any way three hooks could pass all the way through Pal without getting caught somewhere.

I felt like I was going to throw up, but Pal's bouncing around and wanting to play the same as always helped me to slowly recover my composure.

After considerable thought, I finally decided that Pal and I would keep our secret and see what happened.

I didn't fish any more that day and on the way walking home, I watched Pal's every move. He chased grasshoppers and birds the same as always, but I just felt it was too soon for any effects to start showing from the hooks.

I well imagine I was kind of quiet at the supper table that night and when Gramps asked about catfishing, I felt my face flush, and I was sure he could tell something was wrong.

The last thing I did was to check Pal before I went to bed and he was sound asleep on his favorite rug in front of the kitchen door.

I had a difficult time going to sleep that night. Maybe it was because I spent a lot of time praying. I remember waking many times, damp from horrid dreams of Pal and many weird disasters resulting from the hooks.

I was awake early and lay there listening to see if Gramps was up yet. Everything was dreadfully and scary quiet. I wanted to get up but was afraid to look out on the kitchen rug for fear I would find Pal stretched out dead.

After awhile, I heard the kitchen door open. The next thing I heard was Gramps say, "Well, you coming in or staying out?"

A thrill shot through my body as I heard Pal's toenails clicking on the well-worn linoleum kitchen floor. He was alive and about.

I bounded out of bed, slipped into my pants, and the minute Pal heard me, he was halfway to my bedroom when I came out. Pal was his joyful self and to me, one of the most welcome sights I had ever had the pleasure of greeting.

We went fishing again and I watched Pal continuously for signs of distress of any kind. I felt if Pal could get through another day and night, maybe things would be okay.

Every time Pal had a bowel movement, I checked it for blood and hooks, but neither showed up.

When I got up the second morning and was again met by Pal in his same energetic fashion, the heavy weight was lifted from my shoulders.

Pal and I spent many happy days together. We never shared our secret of the catfish bait and hooks with anyone.

I will never know what happened to the hooks, but one thing for sure, those were two of the most stressful days and nights a twelve-year-old boy could ever experience.

10
CONCLUSION

Conclusion

I am now sixty-three years old and it has been over forty years since I last saw the farm that played such an important part of this book. The buildings have remained unused this same amount of time. I don't think I would want to see the farm again. I want to remember it only as it was when I grew up. The deteriorated changes now would be too difficult to face.

All the sounds would now be gone, as would the associated sights that went with them. They once lived together, one depending on and relating to the other.

The rain pounding on the tin roof of the porch could only properly be heard from the adjoining bedroom at night.

The squealing of the pigs could only be heard when they fought over a shovel of corn or a pail of slop Dad fed them.

The bawling of a newborn calf and its mother could only be heard when Dad separated the two.

The yard gate slamming with a spring-tensioned slap was only heard when someone passed through it.

The rattling of the milk cans and pails only occurred when Mother washed them.

The noise of the chickens was continuous as a result of laying eggs or being frightened by a red-tailed hawk.

The slow, mournful put-put-put of the one-cylinder engine on Mom's washing machine could be heard throughout the farm on a quiet day.

The smell of fresh baked bread and frying pork was the result of Mom getting another delicious meal.

The barking of Jimmy excitingly announced we were having company.

The rattling of the iron-wheeled horse-drawn machinery running over the rocks in the barnyard road told us Dad was nearby.

The sounds of laughing with joy or crying with unhappiness were a normal result of children playing.

The rattling of the dipper in the drinking pail told us someone was getting a drink.

These were all friendly, comforting, good sounds. Without them, an important part of the farm would now be missing.

These sounds, smells, and sights vividly remain in my memory, and that is how I wish to remember our "hardscrabble" farm.

To order additional copies of this book,
please send full amount plus $4.00 for
postage and handling for the first book and
50¢ for each additional book.

Send orders to:

Galde Press, Inc.
PO Box 460
Lakeville, Minnesota 55044-0460

Credit card orders call 1–800–777–3454
Phone (612) 891-5991 • Fax (612) 891-6091
Visit our website at http://www.galdepress.com
e-mail: pgalde@minn.net

Write for our free catalog.